Baedeker Berlin

D0284086

Imprint

Cover picture: Emperor William Memorial Church

88 colour photographs
11 plans, 3 drawings, 1 transport plan (U- and S-Bahn), 1 large city map

Conception and editorial work:
Redaktionsbüro Harenberg, Schwerte
English Language: Alec Court

Text: Marianne Bernhard
Revision and additional text: Baedeker Editorial Department

General direction:
Dr Peter Baumgarten, Baedeker Stuttgart

Cartography:
Ingenieurbüro für Kartographie Huber & Oberländer, Munich
Georg Schiffner, Lahr (panoramic view of Unter den Linden)
Richard Schwarz Nachf., Berlin (city map)

English translation:
James Hogarth

Source of illustrations:
Bröhan Museum (2), Europahaus (1), Historia-Photo (15), Kappelmeyer (13), König (3), Lammel (2), Lehnartz (39), Mauritius (1), Messerschmidt (1), Prenzel (1), Sperber (1), Uthoff (9)

Following the tradition established by Karl Baedeker in 1844, sights of particular interest and hotels or restaurants of particular quality are distinguished by either one or two asterisks.

To make it easier to locate the various sights listed in the "A to Z" section of the Guide, their coordinates on the large map of Berlin (and on the smaller inset plan) are shown in red at the head of each entry, and the nearest U-Bahn (Underground) and S-Bahn (suburban) stations and most convenient bus services are given.

Only a selection of hotels, restaurants and shops can be given: no reflection is implied, therefore, on establishments not included.

In a time of rapid change it is difficult to ensure that all the information given is entirely accurate and up to date, and the possibility of error can never be entirely eliminated. Although the publishers can accept no responsibility for inaccuracies and omissions, they are always grateful for corrections and suggestions for improvement.

Contents

Page

The Principal Sights at a Glance . . . . inside front cover

Plan of U- and S-Bahn (underground) 6

Preface 7

Facts and Figures. 9

General 9

Population and Religion. 10

Transport 10

Culture 13

Commerce and Industry 15

Noted Berlin Figures 15

History of Berlin 21

Sectors and Wards of Berlin 24

Hohenzollern Rulers of Brandenburg and Prussia 25

West Berlin from A to Z 26

East Berlin 91

General 91

Transport 91

Culture 91

Commerce and Industry 91

Entry Points from West Berlin 93

East Berlin from A to Z 94

Practical Information 132

Useful Telephone Numbers 167

City Map . . . . at end of book

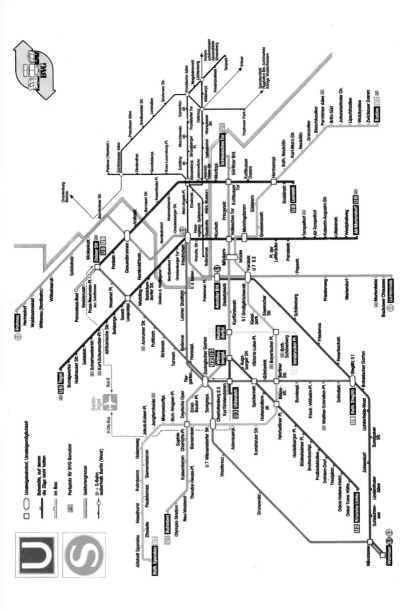

Preface

This Pocket Guide to Berlin is one of the new generation of Baedeker city guides.

Baedeker pocket guides, illustrated throughout in colour, are designed to meet the needs of the modern traveller. They are quick and easy to consult, with the principal features of interest described in alphabetical order and practical details about location, opening times, etc., shown in the margin.

Each guide is divided into three parts. The first part gives a general account of the city, its history, notable personalities and so on; in the second part the principal sights are described; and the third part contains a variety of practical information designed to help visitors to find their way about and make the most of their stay.

The new guides are abundantly illustrated and contain numbers of newly drawn plans. At the back of the book is a large city map, and each entry in the main part of the guide gives the coordinates of the square on the map in which the particular feature can be located. Users of this guide, therefore, will have no difficulty in finding what they want to see.

Facts and Figures

Arms of the
City of Berlin

General

Berlin is the largest city in Germany, with a total area of 883 sq. km (341 sq. miles). Capital of the German Reich from 1871 to 1945, it was divided after the Second World War into West Berlin and East Berlin.

The city

Under Article 1 of the Berlin Constitution of 1950 Berlin is a German province (*Land*) and a German city. Under Article 23 of the Basic Law (Constitution) of the Federal Republic of Germany West Berlin is regarded as belonging to the Federal Republic. It occupies a special position, however, since ultimate authority rests with the American, British and French Commandants in their respective sectors, although it is within the economic sphere, and uses the currency, of the Federal Republic. The *Land* of West Berlin is a democratically governed city state.
East Berlin has been declared, with the concurrence of the Soviet Union, capital of the German Democratic Republic (GDR).

Political status

Latitude 52° 31′ N; Longitude 13° 25′ E.

Geographical situation

From the United Kingdom to West Berlin: 010 49 30
From the United States or Canada to West Berlin: 011 49 30
From the United Kingdom to East Berlin: 010 37 2
From the United States or Canada to East Berlin: 011 37 2

Telephone dialing codes

Greater Berlin has an area of 883 sq. km (341 sq. miles), 480 sq. km (185 sq. miles; 54·4 per cent) in West Berlin and 403 sq. km (156 sq. miles; 45·6 per cent) in East Berlin. The population is some 3·1 million, 1·9 million in West Berlin and 1·2 million in East Berlin. More than a third of the area of West Berlin is built up.

Area and population

West Berlin:
Kreuzberg, Tiergarten, Wedding, Neukölln, Tempelhof, Schöneberg, Steglitz, Charlottenburg, Wilmersdorf, Zehlendorf, Reinickendorf, Spandau.

City wards (*Bezirke*)

East Berlin:
Mitte, Prenzlauer Berg, Friedrichshain, Pankow, Weissensee, Lichtenberg, Treptow, Köpenick.

See map on p. 24.

Under a provision of the 1950 Constitution (suspended) West Berlin became a *Land* (province) of the Federal Republic of Germany; it is represented in the West German Parliament by four members of the Bundesrat and 22 members of the Bundestag, without the power to vote. The city has a

Administration

◀ *The Kurfürstendamm, with the Emperor William Memorial Church and the Europa Center*

9

parliament of its own, the House of Representatives (Abgeord-netenhaus); executive power rests with the Senate, headed by the Chief Burgomaster (Regierender Bürgermeister).

East Berlin, which according to international law is not part of the German Democratic Republic, is nevertheless designated as its capital. It is governed by a municipal council (Magistrat) headed by a Senior Burgomaster (Oberbürgermeister).

Population and Religion

Population

The population of Berlin is a mixture of old-established Berliners and incomers from other German territories, together with non-Germans who found their way to Berlin over the centuries, sometimes recruited to work there, sometimes of their own free will (Dutch workers, Huguenots, etc.).

The steady influx of new people brought the Berliners into contact with a variety of different religious beliefs, philosophies and manners and customs, developing in them the adaptability and the tolerance which made coexistence possible. This tolerance is still a Berlin characteristic, so that incomers and visitors are not made to feel themselves as strangers.

Berlin reached its population peak in 1943, when it had 4·5 million inhabitants. Immediately after the last war the population had shrunk to 2·5 million.

The stream of refugees from the German Democratic Republic and the return of families which had been evacuated during the war led to a steady increase in the population of West Berlin from 1945 to 1957. The construction of the Berlin Wall in 1961 had a dramatic effect on the growth of West Berlin: the inflow of refugees dwindled to a mere trickle, producing an unfavourable population structure with a steadily increasing proportion of older people.

In East Berlin, on the other hand, the continuing outflow of refugees (100,000 between 1950 and 1960) led to a steady decline in population; though since 1961 there has been a slight but continuous rising trend.

Religion

The population of West Berlin, apart from the foreign "guest workers", is predominantly Protestant, but the city has numerous Roman Catholic as well as Protestant churches (see Practical Information, Churches), together with synagogues and places of worship for other religious communities.

Transport

As a result of political circumstances and the division of the city since the war, Berlin has lost much of its former importance, but it is still a considerable centre of communications by land, air and water.

Road traffic

West Berlin has about 670,000 registered vehicles (*c.* 5000 taxis). The road network comprises about 2900 km (1800 miles), including more than 40 km (25 miles) of urban

City motorway, with Radio Tower ▶

highways. The roads are notable for their breadth – even those dating from the age of horse traffic being generously planned. This inheritance from the past, combined with the planning of the post-war years, has enabled Berlin to escape the chaos produced by rush-hour traffic in other large cities.

Rail services

Berlin formerly had the busiest rail traffic of any German city, with 500 trains arriving or leaving every day. West Berlin now has only one long-distance station (Zoo Station), with a daily traffic of 28 passenger trains each way, providing communications with towns in the German Democratic Republic and with the Soviet Union, Czechoslovakia, Poland, Austria, Hungary, etc.

East Berlin has two large long-distances stations (Friedrichstrasse and the Ostbahnhof or Eastern Station), with services to and from the Zoo Station in West Berlin, the Federal Republic, Italy, Copenhagen, etc.

Airports

In view of Berlin's isolated situation air services are of particular importance in the movement of passenger traffic. The city's original airport was Tempelhof, but since Tempelhof's central situation made it impossible to extend the runways, the decision was taken to develop Tegel, on the northern outskirts of the city, as West Berlin's principal airport. The new airport, opened in 1974, has two runways – 3000 m (3280 yd) and 2400 m (2625 yd) long – which can handle Jumbo jets. There are 14 passenger gangways, and the apron can accommodate some 30 aircraft. There are bus services (No. 9) to and from Budapester Strasse via the Zoo Station and (No. 8) from the U-Bahn station Osloer Strasse and a direct link with the city highway.

East Berlin's main airport is Schönefeld.

River ports

Berlin has two main river ports, the Western Port in West Berlin and the Eastern Port in East Berlin. Much of Berlin's freight traffic, both incoming (primarily raw materials and semi-finished products) and outgoing (finished products), travels by water, on the Oder-Spree, Teltow and Oder-Havel Canals.

Municipal transport

Most of the passenger traffic within the city is carried by the U-Bahn (Underground) and the buses run by the municipal transport authority, the Berliner Verkehrs-Betriebe (BVG).
The U-Bahn system was developed further after the building of the Berlin Wall in 1961 in order to handle traffic previously carried by the much-used S-Bahn (suburban) system run by the GDR State Railways until 1983. For the most part the lines run in tunnels, but there are some sections in cuttings or on elevated tracks.
Since 1984 the S-Bahn lines in West Berlin have been run by the West Berlin BVG.
The buses are mostly double-deckers. Berlin's electric trams – the oldest electric tramway system in Germany, originally established, with horse traction, in 1865 – ceased to run in West Berlin in 1967.

In East Berlin both trams and buses are in operation.

Free University of Berlin

Culture

West Berlin has two universities, the Free University in Dahlem, founded in 1948, and the University of Technology in Charlottenburg, established in 1879. There are also the National College of Art (with nine departments), the College of Education, the College of Theology, the European College of Economics and a large number of research institutes, including the Hahn-Meitner Institute of Nuclear Research. East Berlin has the Humboldt University.

Universities, etc.

The Opera House (Deutsche Oper Berlin) in West Berlin, in a new building erected in 1961, is one of the leading opera-houses of the Western World. Performances are given every evening, with occasional programmes of ballet.
The Theater des Westens puts on operettas and musicals, and from time to time there are also performances of "chamber music" or international ballet at the Tribüne and in the Academy of Arts.
In addition to the world-famous Berlin Philharmonic Orchestra, with its equally famous conductor Herbert von Karajan, there are the fine Radio Symphony Orchestra of Berlin, the Berlin Symphony Orchestra, the Berlin Baroque Orchestra, the Academy of Singing, the choir of St Hedwig's Cathedral and a variety of other ensembles.
East Berlin also has its Opera House, housing the old-established German National Opera (Deutsche Staatsoper),

Music

Berlin Philharmonic Orchestra

with its excellent orchestra, the Staatskapelle Berlin. The Comic Opera in East Berlin also has a high reputation.

Drama

West Berlin has three fine State theatres, directed by Heribert Sasse – the Schiller-Theater, its associated Theatre Workshop (Schiller-Theater Werkstatt) and the Schlosspark-Theatre in Steglitz – as well as numerous privately run theatres, notable among them the Schaubühne in Lehniner Platz.
East Berlin has the internationally known Berliner Ensemble, founded by Bertolt Brecht in 1949.

Festivals

Berlin is a leading festival city. Among the most interesting events are:
The Berlin Festival, held annually in autumn. Established six years after the war, it offers a cross-section of international achievement in all fields of art.
The Berlin International Film Festival, established in 1951 and now held annually in February–March. The latest films from all over the world are judged by an international jury and the best are awarded the Gold and Silver Bear (the bear being Berlin's heraldic animal).
The Berlin Drama Meeting (Theatertreffen Berlin), held annually in May, when a jury of ten critics select the ten best German-language productions of the preceding year.
The Festival of World Cultures, first held in the summer of 1979, which presents the cultural achievements of non-European countries.
The International Summer Festival, an open-air festival of "happenings", music and drama first held in 1978.
The Berlin Jazz Days, a festival lasting five days, established by

Joachim-Ernst Behrendt and held annually in autumn, which gives a survey of the history, present state and avant-garde of jazz.

Other festivals include the Television Competition, held in alternate years, and Interdrama (every three years).

The dates of the various festivals vary from year to year.

Commerce and Industry

In spite of the dismantling of many factories after the last war and the city's isolated situation, West Berlin is still the largest industrial centre in Germany.

West Berlin's major industrial effort is devoted to the production of capital goods, with the electrical industry taking a leading place. The most important firms in this field are Siemens, AEG-Telefunken and Osram. The second place in the industrial hierarchy is occupied by engineering and motor-vehicle manufacture, which are followed by the foodstuff, chemical, clothing and tobacco industries.

Traditional industries

After industry the largest employers of labour are commerce, banking and insurance.

The importance of Berlin as a national and international centre is reflected in the numerous congresses, conferences, exhibitions and other events held in the city and now catered for by the huge complex of the International Congress Centre.

Commerce and service trades

Noted Berlin Figures

The "Iron Chancellor", founder of the German Empire in 1871, came of a noble family with estates in Pomerania and Brandenburg. After studying at Göttingen and Berlin he became a civil servant, but found the work unsatisfying and soon retired to manage the family estates. After his father's death he became a member of the Provincial Diet, in which he showed himself a staunch conservative. He went on to become a member of the Prussian United Diet and Prussian Ambassador in St Petersburg and Paris. In 1862 he was appointed Chancellor (Prime Minister) and Foreign Minister of Prussia, and in 1871 became first Chancellor of the German Empire which his policies had helped to create. He was dismissed by William II in 1890.

Otto von Bismarck (1815–98)

Bismarck, a man of choleric and autocratic disposition, was nevertheless very popular in Berlin. After initial difficulties he won general respect within Prussia, even from his opponents, and retained his popularity with the people of Berlin even after his fall.

Brecht began by studing medicine in Munich, and served as a medical orderly in the First World War, but soon turned to the theatre. In 1924 he went to Berlin, where he worked with Max Reinhardt at the Deutsches Theater. In 1928 he became a convert to Marxism. In 1933 he left Germany, and after

Bertolt Brecht (1898–1956)

15

spending some time in Switzerland, Denmark and Moscow found his way to America. In 1947 he settled in Zürich, and in the following year moved to East Berlin, where, in association with his wife, the actress Helene Weigel, he founded his own theatre, the famous Berliner Ensemble.

Brecht's plays are works of social and political criticism, didactic in intent and much concerned with the class struggle and the plight of the poor, the under-privileged and the exploited. His best-known works are "The Threepenny Opera" (1928; written in collaboration with Kurt Weill), "Mother Courage and her Children" (1941), "The Good Woman of Setzuan" (1943) and "The Caucasian Chalk Circle" (1955).

Daniel Nikolaus Chodowiecki (1726–1801)

Chodowiecki was one of the leading etchers and engravers of the Rococo period, noted particularly for his etchings of scenes from everyday life in Frederick the Great's Prussia, drawn with a touch of gentle irony. He also worked as an illustrator, mostly of plays (Lessing, Goethe, Schiller, etc.) but also of scientific works (Lavater, Basedow). Some 2000 of his etchings, and as many drawings, have been preserved. Examples of his work can be seen in the Print Cabinet of the Dahlem Museums.

Theodor Fontane (1819–98)

Educated in Berlin, Fontane was trained as a pharmacist, but soon turned to writing as a part-time and later a full-time occupation. He spent some years in Britain as correspondent of German newspapers and then returned to Berlin. In his later years he wrote a number of notable novels, including "Effi Briest" (1895) and "Der Stechlin" (1899). His novels depict 19th c. life in Berlin and the surrounding area, and his "Wanderings in the March of Brandenburg" are lovingly detailed accounts of the landscape and history of this region.

Frederick II, the Great (1712–86)

Frederick, third King of Prussia, came to the throne in 1740. In contrast to his severe and matter-of-fact father, Frederick William I, he had artistic and intellectual interests, corresponded with Voltaire and was both a performer and a composer of music. In 1730, with the help of his friend Lieutenant von Katte, he set out to flee to England but was caught, put on trial by his father and forced to be present at the execution of his friend. Thereafter Frederick conformed to his father's wishes, married and, becoming king, liked to call himself the "first servant of the State". In his early years he did much building in and around Berlin (Rheinsberg Palace, Opera House, Sanssouci), but from the beginning of his reign he was involved in war. This was the time of the Silesian Wars, the Seven Years War, the Partition of Poland, the break with the Habsburgs; but it was also the period of the Enlightenment, of which Frederick was a great admirer and exponent.

Frederick the Great, familiar in his later years as "der alte Fritz", was the subject of many anecdotes, such as the story of the miller of Sanssouci (see A to Z, Potsdam), though he never became a popular figure.

Frederick William, the Great Elector (1620–88)

Frederick William (Friedrich Wilhelm) became Elector of Brandenburg in 1640. During his reign the Duchy of Prussia gained in strength, and in 1675 he won the decisive Battle of Fehrbellin with the Swedes. After Louis XIV's Revocation of the Edict of Nantes Frederick William's Edict of Potsdam in the same year allowed the French Huguenots to settle in Prussia, leading to a growth of industry and manufactures. He imposed

Otto von Bismarck

Bertolt Brecht

Theodor Fontane

a heavy tax burden on his people, but with the revenue thus acquired he rebuilt the Prussian Army, developed the civil service of Prussia and evolved a firm foreign policy.

Alexander von Humboldt, a native of Berlin, was a great traveller, geographer and botanist, a pioneer of agricultural science, meteorology, oceanography and plant geography. After travelling widely in Europe he entered the Prussian Department of Mines, but resigned his appointment to undertake a long journey of exploration in South America with the French botanist Aimé Bonpland (1799–1804). After his return he lived for many years in Paris, but in 1827 returned to Berlin, lectured at the Frederick William University founded by his brother Wilhelm, and in 1829 took part in a scientific expedition in Asiatic Russia. Between 1845 and 1862 his principal work, "Der Kosmos", a description of the physical world was published.

Alexander von Humboldt (1769–1859)

Born in Potsdam, Wilhelm von Humboldt studied law and after extensive travels in Europe worked in the Prussian Ministry of the Interior. While Head of the Education Department he was instrumental in founding the Frederick William University in Berlin in 1810. He was interested in language and in aesthetics, and after retiring from the public service in 1819 devoted himself to linguistic studies.

Wilhelm von Humboldt (1767–1835)

Jahn is famous in Germany as the founder of gymnastics, which he saw as a means of developing the fitness of the young people of Prussia during the Napoleonic Wars. He established the first gymnasium at Hasenheide in Berlin in 1811.
After the defeat of Napoleon Jahn's outspoken views made him unpopular with the Government. He was arrested in 1819 and imprisoned on suspicion of subversive activities, and the practice of gymnastics was prohibited.

Friedrich Jahn (1778–1852)

Kleist came of a military family and served for a time in the Prussian Army, but resigned his commission to study philosophy and mathematics. Thereafter he led a restless and unsettled life, in the course of which he wrote a number of notable plays and short stories. His "Der zerbrochene Krug"

Heinrich von Kleist (1777–1811)

17

Noted Berlin Figures

Frederick William

Wilhelm von Humboldt

Alexander von Humboldt

("The Broken Pitcher") is one of the finest German comedies, and his "Prinz Friedrich von Homburg" expresses the very spirit of Prussia. A basically unstable character, he committed suicide in 1811 on the shores of the Wannsee together with Henriette Vogel.

Georg Wenzeslaus von Knobelsdorff (1699–1753)

One of the leading German architects of the Rococo period, Knobelsdorff was a friend of the young Crown Prince Frederick, later Frederick the Great, for whom he built Rheinsberg Palace and (after his accession to the throne) the Opera House in Berlin. He was also a landscape-architect, laying out the parks of Rheinsberg and Sanssouci and the Lustgarten in Potsdam. His best-known work was Sanssouci Palace (1745–47), based on a first sketch by Frederick himself.

Carl Gotthard Langhans (1732–1808)

A native of Silesia, Langhans was one of the earliest exponents of the Neo-Classical style of architecture in Germany. He was appointed Chief Court Architect in Berlin in 1788, and in 1788–91 created his principal work, the Brandenburg Gate. Other buildings for which he was responsible in and around Berlin include the Old Theatre in the Gendarmenmarkt and the Charlottenburg Theatre, part of the Dutch Palace and the Bellevue Palace, and the interior of the Marble Palace at Potsdam.

Ernst Theodor Litfass (1816–74)

Litfass, a Berlin printer, is notable as the inventor of the "Litfass columns" (Litfassäulen) which still bear his name – cylindrical columns between 8 and 12 feet high on which posters and other advertisements could be pasted.

Adolph von Menzel (1815–1905)

Adolph von Menzel was a largely self-taught painter and graphic artist of the German Realist school. The paintings he produced in the 1840s and 1850s anticipated the work of the Impressionists. A fashionable portrait-painter, he gained fame and a variety of honours, and became something of a Berlin institution, an habitué of its cafés and a guest in its great houses.

Friedrich Nicolai (1733–1811)

The son of a Berlin bookseller, Nicolai carried on his father's business and himself became a writer. His bookshop became

Friedrich Nicolai

Gottfried Schadow

Karl Friedrich Schinkel

the intellectual centre of the Enlightenment in Berlin. In his later years he was a fierce opponent of the new Romantic school.

A French painter who was appointed Prussian Court Painter in 1711. Although he travelled in Germany and to London and Paris, most of his work was done in Berlin and the palaces in the surrounding area, where he painted frescoes and murals as well as easel-pictures. He was patronised by Frederick the Great when Crown Prince, and produced a famous double portrait of Frederick and his sister in the park at Sanssouci, now in Charlottenburg Palace. Other works by Pesne can be seen in Grunewald Hunting Lodge.

Antoine Pesne
(1683–1757)

A typical representative of the Berlin school of Neo-Classical sculpture, Rauch came to the capital in 1797 and worked for a time in Gottfried Schadow's workshop. Thereafter he spent several years in Rome, where he met Thorvaldsen, Canova and Christian Friedrich Tieck, who strongly influenced him. Among Rauch's most notable works were the marble tomb of Queen Luise in the Mausoleum of Charlottenburg Palace and the equestrian statue of Frederick the Great in Unter den Linden.

Christian Daniel Rauch
(1777–1857)

Ernst Reuter became a member of the Berlin City Council in 1926 and was responsible for the establishment of the municipal transport authority, BVG. He was elected to the Reichstag in 1932, but left Germany after Hitler came to power in the following year. Returning to Berlin in 1947, he was elected Senior Burgomaster, but was prevented from taking up office until 1948 by a Soviet veto. From 1950 to 1953 he was Chief Burgomaster of Berlin.

Ernst Reuter
(1889–1953)

Schadow, the leading member of the German Neo-Classical school of sculpture, was trained in Rome and in 1788 became Head of the Court Sculpture Workshop. In 1805 he became Deputy Director and in 1815 Director of the Academy in Berlin. His principal work was the Quadriga on the Brandenburg Gate (1789), but he was also noted for his very personal and realistic portrait sculpture, including the double likeness of the Princesses Luise and Friederike of Prussia (1795–97), which aroused Court displeasure by its frankness and truth to life.

Gottfried Schadow
(1764–1850)

Noted Berlin Figures

Karl Friedrich Schinkel
(1781–1841)

Trained as an architect in Berlin, Schinkel travelled widely in Europe before returning to Berlin. From 1806 to 1810 he worked mainly as a landscape-painter; thereafter he was much concerned with the preservation of historic buildings, and also gained some reputation as a stage-designer before settling down to his profession as an architect in 1817, producing such notable works of Neo-Classical architecture as the Neue Wache in Unter den Linden, the New Theatre in the Gendarmenmarkt, the Old Museum and the Nikolaikirche in Potsdam.

Andreas Schlüter
(1660–1714)

One of the leading German Baroque architects, Schlüter left his imprint on the Baroque architecture of Berlin, to which he came in 1694, working both as an architect and a sculptor. In 1696 he went to Italy, where he became familiar with the Baroque architecture of Michelangelo and Bramante and with Italian sculpture. This influence is reflected in the 21 masks of dying warriors in the courtyard of the Arsenal in Unter den Linden – works of great individuality and expressive force – and in his equestrian statue of the Great Elector (1700), now in the Grand Courtyard of Charlottenburg Palace.

From 1698 to 1707 Schlüter was responsible for the rebuilding of the Palace in Berlin, remodelling its heterogeneous architecture into a harmonious whole in Roman Baroque style. The collapse of the badly designed Mint Tower, however, brought him into disfavour, and he was obliged to resign his post as Court Architect.

Schlüter's other work included the Court Stables (Marstall) in Berlin, the Old Post Office and some works of sculpture, such as the famous bronze bust of Landgrave Frederick II of Hesse-Homburg (1704).

Carl Friedrich Zelter
(1758–1832)

Zelter began by earning his living as a builder, but his real career lay in music. A composer of the Romantic school, he became Director of the Singing Academy and was the teacher of such famous composers as Mendelssohn, Nicolai and Meyerbeer. He was a lifelong friend of Goethe, many of whose poems he set to music.

Heinrich Zille
(1858–1929)

A skilled draughtsman and caricaturist, Zille became the chronicler of the low life and poorer classes of Berlin, contributing regularly to the satirical journals of the day. With all his humour and his sharp eye for a comic situation, he was an acute social critic and a champion of the poor and under-privileged.

History of Berlin

Chronology

Albert (Albrecht) the Bear, of the Ascanian dynasty of Brandenburg, becomes Margrave of the Northern March (Nordmark).	1134
Margraves John and Otto III grant municipal charters to the settlements of Cölln and Berlin.	About 1230
Cölln first appears in the records as a town.	1237
First reference to Berlin as a town.	1244
Berlin and Cölln build a joint Town Hall.	1307
The Ascanian dynasty dies out.	1320
Berlin becomes a member of the Hanseatic League.	1359
Frederick VI, Burgrave of Nuremberg, is appointed Governor of the March of Brandenburg (Mark Brandenburg) by Emperor Sigismund.	1411
Frederick VI recovers territory seized by two marauding nobles, Johann and Dietrich Quitzow.	1414
Frederick VI is granted by the Emperor the March of Brandenburg and the title of Elector.	1415
Elector Frederick II begins building a castle at Cölln.	1443
The citizens of Cölln and Berlin rebel against Frederick's limitation of their privileges, but Frederick represses the rebellion: the first victory of the ruling house over the independence of the towns. Berlin is developed as the Electoral capital.	1448
Elector Joachim III adopts the Reformed faith.	1539
Plague rages in Berlin.	1576
Brandenburg is ravaged by the Thirty Years War. The population is reduced by half – only 12,000 in 1618.	1618–48
Reign of the Great Elector, Frederick William. He gives a powerful impulse to the development of the town: Berlin is fortified and the districts of Friedrichswerder, Dorotheenstadt and Friedrichstadt are built.	1640–88
The construction of the Oder–Spree Canal makes Berlin an important port on the waterway between Hamburg and Breslau.	1662–68
In the decisive Battle of Fehrbellin Frederick William's troops, commanded by Field-Marshal Wrangel, defeat the Swedish	28 June 1675

	force which had thrust into western Brandenburg during the Franco-Dutch War (1672–79).
1685	Edict of Potsdam, permitting the settlement of French Huguenots in Berlin and allowing them to build their own church and school.
1701	Elector Frederick III, son of the Great Elector, crowns himself in Königsberg as first King of Prussia (Frederick I).
1713–40	Reign of Frederick William I, the "Soldier King". He is compelled to economise, since his predecessor Frederick I had left the Treasury empty, but contrives to enlarge the Army, press on with the fortification of Berlin, erect public buildings and dwelling-houses and promote the establishment of schools. This is a period of strict moral standards and a Spartan way of life, both at the Court and among the citizens.
1740–86	Reign of Frederick II, the Great, during which Berlin becomes a European capital.
1745	Sanssouci Palace is built by Georg Wenzeslaus von Knobelsdorff.
1750	New cotton and silk factories are established. Berlin becomes the largest textile town in Germany.
About 1800	With a population of 200,000, Berlin is the third largest city in Europe (after London and Paris).
27 Oct. 1806	Napoleon marches into Berlin: the beginning of three years of French occupation.
1810	Wilhelm von Humboldt founds the Frederick William University.
1811	Friedrich Ludwig Jahn establishes the first gymnasium at Hasenheide.
1838	First railway line, from Berlin to Potsdam.
1839	First horse-drawn omnibus (Alexanderplatz–Potsdamer Platz).
18 Mar. 1848	After street fighting with the garrison the "March Revolution" breaks out in Berlin. Frederick William IV, the "Romantic on the throne of Prussia", cuts a poor figure in face of this bloody rising.
3 Apr. 1849	Frederick William rejects the Imperial Crown which is offered him by the Frankfurt Parliament.
1861	Accession of King William I.
1862	Otto von Bismarck becomes Chancellor (Prime Minister) of Prussia.
18 Jan. 1871	Proclamation of the German Emperor in the Hall of Mirrors at Versailles. Berlin becomes the Imperial capital; King William I becomes Emperor.

Electric lighting comes to Berlin, which also has the world's first electric railway.	1879
Telephone service introduced.	1881
Emperor William I dies at the age of 90.	9 Mar. 1888
The "year of the three Emperors": Frederick III reigns for only 99 days and is succeeded by his son, William II.	1888
William II dismisses Bismarck.	20 Mar. 1890
The first Underground line is opened	1902
Philipp Scheidemann proclaims Germany a Republic, seeking to forestall the establishment of a Socialist republic by the Communists.	9 Nov. 1918
Berlin and its suburbs become an enlarged city, divided into 20 wards.	1920
Hitler seizes power.	30 Jan. 1933
The 11th Summer Olympics are held in Berlin.	1936
Second World War. Berlin suffers fearful devastation.	1939–45
The Berlin Blockade. Currency reform in the Western occupation zones of Germany and the Western sectors of Berlin is followed by a similar reform in the Eastern (Soviet) zone and sector. The Soviet Union imposes a blockade on the three Western sectors of Berlin. The American Commandant in Berlin, General Lucius D. Clay, organises the Allied air-lift to bring in essential supplies.	1948–49
Proclamation of the German Democratic Republic, with East Berlin as its capital.	9 Oct. 1949
New Constitution of Berlin. Ernst Reuter becomes the first Chief Burgomaster of West Berlin.	1 Oct. 1950
A rising in East Berlin is repressed by the East German Government with the help of Soviet troops.	17 June 1953
The "Berlin Ultimatum": the Soviet Union demands that West Berlin should become a "free, demilitarised city".	1958
A conference of Foreign Ministers in Geneva fails to solve the Berlin problem. The Soviet Prime Minister, Khrushchev, drops the Berlin Ultimatum.	1959
The East German authorities begin the construction of the Berlin Wall. East Berlin is sealed off from West Berlin, at first by a barbed-wire barrier, then by a concrete wall which is kept under strict military observation and guard.	13 Aug. 1961
The American President, John F. Kennedy, visits West Berlin and declares at Schöneberg Town Hall "I am a Berliner."	26 June 1963

Dec. 1963	Agreement on passes between West and East Berlin: for the first time for 28 months West Berliners are able to visit their relatives in East Berlin.
3 Sept. 1971	Four-Power agreement on Berlin.
1972	Under the Berlin Agreement West Berliners are again permitted to visit East Berlin and East Germany, and transit between West Germany and West Berlin is made much easier.
1980	The German Democratic Republic substantially increases the minimum amounts of Western currency to be exchanged on visits to East Berlin and East Germany. The number of visitors falls by a third.
1981	Election in West Berlin: the Christian Democratic Union fails to get an absolute majority, but nevertheless forms a Government.
1982	The US President, Ronald Reagan visits West Berlin.
1984	The S-Bahn in West Berlin is taken over by the BVG. Natural gas from Russian fields reaches West Berlin.

Sectors and Wards of Berlin

Berlin

West Berlin
French Sector
British Sector
American Sector

East Berlin
Soviet Sector

Reinickendorf
Pankow
Weissensee
Spandau
Wedding
Prenz-lauer Berg
Tier-garten
Mitte
Fried-richs-hain
Charlottenburg
Lichtenberg
Wilmersdorf
Schö-ne-berg
Kreuzberg
Zehlendorf
Steglitz
Tempel-hof
Neukölln
Treptow
Köpenick

City boundary
Boundary between West and East Berlin
Sectoral boundaries in West Berlin
Ward boundaries

Cultural contract between East and West Germany   1986
Centre for Heart Attack research opened in West Berlin

750th Anniversary of Berlin celebrated in both West and East   1987
Berlin

Berlin appointed to be European Culture Metropolitan city   1988

Hohenzollern Rulers of Brandenburg and Prussia

Frederick I	1415–1440	Electors
Frederick II	1440–1470	
Albert Achilles	1470–1486	
John Cicero	1486–1499	
Joachim I Nestor	1499–1535	
Joachim II Hector	1535–1571	
John George	1571–1598	
Joachim Frederick	1598–1608	
John Sigismund	1608–1619	
George William	1619–1640	
Frederick William, the Great Elector	1640–1688	
Frederick III (from 1701 King of Prussia as Frederick I)	1688–1713	
Frederick I	1701–1713	Kings of Prussia
Frederick William I	1713–1740	
Frederick II, the Great	1740–1786	
Frederick William II	1786–1797	
Frederick William III	1797–1840	
Frederick William IV	1840–1861	
William I	1861–1871	
William I	1871–1888	German Emperors
Frederick III	1888	
William II	1888–1918	

West Berlin from A to Z

*Academy of Arts (Akademie der Künste)   B4

Location
Hanseatenweg 10,
Tiergarten

U-Bahn
Hansaplatz

S-Bahn
Bellevue

Buses
16, 23

The Academy of Arts (refounded in 1955) is the successor in West Berlin to the Art Academy of Elector Frederick III, later King Frederick I of Prussia. (The successor to the Academy in East Berlin is the Academy of Arts of the GDR: see that entry.) Frederick and his cultured wife Sophie Charlotte founded the original Academy in 1696 as an institution which should not only develop the skill of artists who had already completed their normal training but should promote communication between artists, art scholars and those interested in the arts: it was to be "a well-ordered academy or school of art and not one of the ordinary painters' or sculptors' academies such as are found everywhere."

As refounded in 1955, the Academy of Arts maintains the tradition of its predecessor, with departments of fine art, sculpture, architecture, music, literature and dramatic art; 1984 saw the establishment of a department of the art of film and media.

The building occupied by the Academy, designed by the Berlin architect Werner Düttmann, was built with funds provided by a German-American, Henry R. Reichhold, in 1960. It has five floors and is divided into three parts, connected by galleries and foyers – the Blaues Haus (Blue House), which contains offices, workrooms, conference rooms and living accommodation; the exhibition building; and the studio building, with a theatre. The Academy puts on periodic exhibitions.

American Memorial Library (Amerika-Gedenkbibliothek)   C5
(Berlin Central Library)

Location:
Blücherplatz

U-Bahn
Hallesches Tor

Buses
24, 41, 95

Opening times
Mon. 4–8 p.m., Tue.–Sat.
11 a.m.–8 p.m.

The United States contributed 5·4 million DM for the building of the Berlin Central Library, commemorating the Berlin Blockade and the American part in the air-lift which enabled the city to withstand the blockade.

With a capacity of some 600,000 volumes the library is one of the largest of the kind in the German Federal Republic and West Berlin. Its present stock comprises 700,000 books, 13,000 volumes of music and 6200 records, together with cassette and tape recordings, slides and 2650 current newspapers, periodicals and annuals.

Aquarium

See Zoo.

Art Library (Kunstbibliot)   B4 (a IV)

The Art Library, one of the State museums of the Stiftung Preussischer Kulturbesitz (Prussian Cultural Heritage Foundation), comprises in addition to the art library proper the Lipperheide Costume Library, a collection of graphic art and a photographic archive. Founded in 1867, it developed out of the Craft Museum of the Berlin Craft Workers' Union (Handwerkerverein).
Adjoining is a museum of architecture and fashion and graphic design.
Opening times: Mon. and Thu. 1–9 p.m., Tue., Wed. and Fri. 9 a.m.–5 p.m.

Location
Jebenstrasse 2,
Charlottenburg

U- and S-Bahn
Zoologischer Garten

Buses
9, 54, 73, 90, 94

Avus   C2/3

The practice driving-track known as Avus (from the initials of the German term Automobil-Verkehrs- und Übungsstrasse) was the first German car-racing circuit, opened in 1921. It consists of two parallel straight stretches some 9 km (5½ miles) long running through the Grunewald (see entry) and ending at Nikolassee.
In 1937 Bernd Rosemeyer established the circuit record of 276·4 km p.h. (171·7 m.p.h.) in an Auto Union and Rudolf

Avus and the International Congress Centre

Caracciola achieved a maximum speed of 400 km p.h. (250 m.p.h.) in a Mercedes.

Nowadays the Avus is mainly of importance as the busiest exit road from Berlin, leading to the Wannsee, the Grunewald and the Dreilinden/Drewitz frontier crossing. Its notorious bends have been straightened out, and it is no longer an international car-racing circuit.

Bellevue Palace (Schloss Bellevue)   B4

Location
Spreeweg, Tiergarten

S-Bahn
Bellevue

Buses
16, 24, 69

Opening times
When the President is not in residence:
Palace only with prior notice (tel. 39 10 51)
Park daily 8 a.m.–dusk

Bellevue Palace, situated to the north-east of the Victory Column (see entry), is the Berlin residence of the President of the Federal Republic and is thus not always open to the public. Bellevue was built in 1785 as a summer palace for Prince Augustus Ferdinand, Frederick the Great's youngest brother. It was destroyed during the Second World War, but was rebuilt after the war, retaining the exterior aspect and general layout of the original palace. The oval reception-room (by C. G. Langhans, 1791) was also restored in its original form; the other rooms were rebuilt in Neo-Classical style.

The western part of the park is landscaped in the English manner. Many of the trees were presented by British people, including the royal family.

Exhibitions and concerts take place in the thatched building in the park. Adjoining is a reading room containing horticultural and zoological literature.

Bellevue Palace

Former building of the Supreme Court in Lindenstrasse, built 1734–35 by Philipp Gerlach, rebuilt 1967–69.

Berlin Museum

A Entrance Hall B Cloakroom C Staircase 00 Toilets

GROUND FLOOR
 1 Berlin and Potsdam 16–18th c.
2–3 Model, plan and views of city until end of 18th c.
 4 Art and craft in the time of Frederick the Great.
 5 Chodowiecki Gallery.
 6 Literary and spiritual life in the 18th c.
 7 Berlin "White Beer" Room.
 8 Berlin faience, porcelain, and silver; Potsdam and Zechlin glass, including 18th c. work.
 9 18th c. paintings and furniture.
10 Judaica.

UPPER FLOOR
11 Berlin metal-casting in the 19th c.
12 Berlin iron-casting of the 19th c.
13 Berlin silver of the 19th c.
14 Textile design of the 18th and 19th c., the Wagler Posamentier studio.
15 Berlin portrait gallery, 19th c.
16 Birth of the middle-class city in the 19th c.
17 Townscape of Berlin in the 19th c. (models, pictures, drawings).
18– Berlin home décor from about
21 1800.

22 Berlin in the 20th c.
23 Paintings of Berlin Secessionists.

TOP FLOOR
(not on plan)
Humorous drawings of Berlin.
Berlin fashions from 19th to 20th c.
Toys and dolls' houses.
Coins and medals.
Berlin intarsia firm "Nast".

STAIRCASE
(six sections)
C Views of Berlin and its surroundings.

*Berlin Museum   C5

The Berlin Museum has been housed since 1968 in the old Supreme Court (Kammergericht) building, designed by the Berlin architect Philipp Gerlach in 1734–35 during the reign of Frederick William I, to accommodate the judicial and administrative authorities which had hitherto occupied part of the Royal Palace. Destroyed during the Second World War, it was rebuilt in 1967–69.

The collection illustrates the history and culture of Berlin since the mid 17th c. Notable exhibits include views of Berlin, postcards designs, Berlin arts and crafts and home décor, portraits, and toys made in Berlin. The museum also contains an exhibition of work by the well-known painter of Berlin life Heinrich Zille. Periodic special exhibitions are mounted throughout the year.

The museum has a bierstube (public bar) where visitors can

Location
Lindenstr. 14, Kreuzberg

U-Bahn
Hallesches Tor

Buses
24, 29, 41, 95

Opening times
Tue.–Sun. 11 a.m.–6 p.m.
Closed 1 April

Botanic Gardens

refresh themselves with a glass of weissbier (the light fizzy beer which is popular in Berlin).

---

*Botanic Gardens and Botanical Museum C3/4
(Botanischer Garten und Botanisches Museum)

Location
Königin-Luise-Str. 6–8,
Steglitz

S-Bahn
Botanischer Garten

Buses
1, 17, 48

Opening times
Summer, daily 9 a.m.–7 p.m.;
Winter, 9 a.m. to dusk;
hothouses close earlier

Botanical Museum

Opening times
Tue.–Sun. 10 a.m.–5 p.m.
(Wed. 10 a.m.–7 p.m.)

Closed
Mon.

The Botanic Gardens, laid out by Adolf Engler between 1897 and 1909, contain within their 42 hectares (104 acres) some 18,000 species of plants grouped on scientific principles: thus there are a series of open beds arranged geographically, a wooded area, a section devoted to useful and medicinal plants and a series of tropical houses (in particular the Victoria House) and a garden where blind people can smell and touch the plants.

Apart from their value for teaching and research, the Botanic Gardens are a very popular place of recreation for the people of Berlin.

The Museum has a herbarium with some $1\frac{1}{2}$ million plants and a large specialised library.

A particular feature of the museum is its display collection. Here visitors can test – or extend – their botanical knowledge, for example by trying to identify trees by their leaves. There is also an interesting series of dioramas showing the earth as it appeared in primeval times.

Bröhan Museum

B3

The Bröhan Museum, opened in 1983 on the ground floor of a former infantry barracks, houses the private collection of Professor Karl H. Bröhan which he donated to the City of Berlin.

There are some 1600 exhibits, which include paintings, graphics, sculptures, furniture, porcelain and ceramics, glass, pewter and silver, dating from 1890 to 1940. The showcases containing selected Art Nouveau and Art Deco objects, but also typical examples of good industrial design, are in rooms in which can be seen valuable French Art Nouveau and Art Deco furniture and carpets of the period. Together with the pictures and sculpture the exhibits provide an excellent impression of the period in question.

The individual rooms bear the names of the furniture-designers whose works are therein exhibited: 1. Porcelain Collection I: Art Nouveau porcelain from Berlin and Copenhagen. 2. Hector Guimard Room: Paintings by Hagemeister, crystal glass of the Loetz firm. 3. Louis Majorelle Room: also furniture by Galle, paintings by Hagemeister and Baluschek. 4–5. Dominique Room: Paintings by Baluschek, Bohemian crystal. 6. Jules Leleu Room: Pictures by various artists. 7. Edgar Brandt Room: Wrought-iron work by Brandt, paintings by Baluschek. 8. Pierre Chareau Room: Paintings by Lambert-Ruckl. 9. Süe et Mare Room: Paintings by Hagemeister and Jaeckel. 10–13. Jacques-Emile Ruhlmann Suite: Paintings by Jaeckel and Lambert-Rucki, objects from the Viennese workshop,

Location
Schloss Strasse 1a
opposite Charlottenburg
Palace

U-Bahn
Richard Wagner Platz

Buses
9, 21, 54, 62, 74, 87

Opening times
Tue.–Sun. 10 a.m.–6 p.m.

L.-M.-B. Latour: "Tänzerin" (c. 1910)   *H. Baluschek: "Tingeltangel" (c. 1900)*

porcelain of the 1920s and 1930s of various manufacturers. Room with high windows: Development of porcelain from Art Nouveau to Functionalism. 15. Treasury: Silver of the 1930s and 1940s, Serapis faience from Vienna, Kayser pewter, Art Deco enamel work. 16. Maurice Dufrene Room: Pictures by Leistikow. 17. Paul Iribe Room: Glass of the 1920s and 1930s. 18. Andre Groult Room: Pictures by Baluschek, Art Nouveau ceramics, eggshell porcelain. 19. Porcelain Collection II: Art Nouveau porcelain from Meissen and Sèvres. Lobby: Paintings and drawings by various artists, faience and stoneware of the 1920s and 1930s, glass from the Art Nouveau period to the 1930s.

---

* Brücke Museum   C3

Location
Bussardsteig 9, Dahlem

Bus
60 (Clayallee/Pücklerstr.)

Opening times
Daily, except Tue., 11 a.m.–
5 p.m.

This low modern building in the Grunewald was built in 1967 by Werner Düttmann, architect of the Academy of Arts (see entry), as a gallery and archive for the works of the group of Expressionist painters known as "Die Brücke" ("The Bridge"). The initiative for the establishment of the museum came from the Berlin artist Karl Schmidt-Rottluff, one of the founders of the group, who presented a large number of his works.

Among other members of the group represented in the museum by paintings, water-colours, drawings and sculpture are Erich Heckel, Ernst Ludwig Kirchner, Otto Mueller and Max Pechstein. The museum also has works by other painters, including Otto Herbig, Max Kaus, Emil Nolde and Emy Röder, who had stylistic or personal affinities with "Die Brücke".

Buckow Church   D5

Location
Alt-Buckow

Buses
52, 91

This little village church was built about 1250. The Early Gothic nave of granite ashlar and the barrel roof date from the original foundation, the Late Gothic ribbed vaulting from the 15th c. Notable features of the church are the chancel windows (by the Berlin craftsman Siegmund Hahn) and the altar cross and liturgical utensils (by Gerhard Schreiter of Bremen).

---

* * Charlottenburg Palace (Schloss Charlottenburg)   B3

Location
Spandauer Damm,
Charlottenburg

U-Bahn
Richard-Wagner-Platz

Buses
9, 21, 54, 62, 74, 87

In 1695 Johann Arnold Nering was commissioned to build a small country house for Sophie Charlotte, wife of the Elector Frederick III. Nering died before the house – known as the "Lietzenburg" after the name of the district in which it lay – was completed, and the work was continued by Schlüter, who was later superseded by his rival Eosander von Göthe, the Electress's favourite.

Schlüter was responsible for the two side wings, built to house the Electoral retinue and servants, since the Elector and his wife planned to spend a good deal of time in the palace. Eosander von Göthe added the projecting element in the centre of the façade in order to provide support for the dome, almost 50 m

Charlottenburg Palace ▶

(165 ft) high, which forms a conspicuous landmark; and in 1709–12 he built the Orangery at the W end of the Palace.

In 1740–46 the New Wing, with a Concert Hall, was built on to the E end of the Palace by Georg Wenzeslaus von Knobelsdorff for Frederick the Great, forming a counterpart to the Orangery. During the reign of Frederick William II a small theatre was built by Carl Gotthard Langhans at the W end of the Orangery (1788–90). The Belvedere tea-house in the park was also built at the time.

The Electress Sophie Charlotte (later first Queen of Prussia) gave brilliant parties and balls in the Palace, which was then still quite small. During the reign of Frederick the Great it provided a magnificent setting for great family celebrations. In the 19th c. Princess Liegnitz, the consort of Frederick William III, and occasionally Frederick William IV lived here.

The façade of the palace is 505 m (1655 ft) long. The golden figure of Fortuna which crowned the dome was destroyed during the Second World War but was replaced after the War by Richard Scheibe. Flanking the entrance gateway of the courtyard are two reproductions of the Borghese "Wrestler".

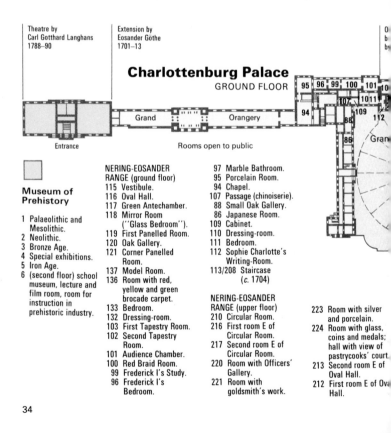

Theatre by
Carl Gotthard Langhans
1788–90

Extension by
Eosander Göthe
1701–13

Charlottenburg Palace
GROUND FLOOR

Grand   Orangery

Entrance   Rooms open to public

Museum of Prehistory

1 Palaeolithic and Mesolithic.
2 Neolithic.
3 Bronze Age.
4 Special exhibitions.
5 Iron Age.
6 (second floor) school museum, lecture and film room, room for instruction in prehistoric industry.

NERING-EOSANDER
RANGE (ground floor)
115 Vestibule.
116 Oval Hall.
117 Green Antechamber.
118 Mirror Room ("Glass Bedroom").
119 First Panelled Room.
120 Oak Gallery.
121 Corner Panelled Room.
137 Model Room.
136 Room with red, yellow and green brocade carpet.
133 Bedroom.
132 Dressing-room.
103 First Tapestry Room.
102 Second Tapestry Room.
101 Audience Chamber.
100 Red Braid Room.
99 Frederick I's Study.
96 Frederick I's Bedroom.

97 Marble Bathroom.
95 Porcelain Room.
94 Chapel.
107 Passage (chinoiserie).
88 Small Oak Gallery.
86 Japanese Room.
109 Cabinet.
110 Dressing-room.
111 Bedroom.
112 Sophie Charlotte's Writing-Room.
113/208 Staircase (c. 1704).

NERING-EOSANDER
RANGE (upper floor)
210 Circular Room.
216 First room E of Circular Room.
217 Second room E of Circular Room.
220 Room with Officers' Gallery.
221 Room with goldsmith's work.

223 Room with silver and porcelain.
224 Room with glass, coins and medals; hall with view of pastrycooks' court.
213 Second room E of Oval Hall.
212 First room E of Oval Hall.

The Palace was severely damaged by air attack on 23 November 1943, but after the war it was rebuilt and most of the interior restored.

The Palace and park are open to the public. In addition to the Historical Apartments the Palace contains the Museum of Prehistory. Features of interest in the park are the Schinkel Pavilion, the Belvedere and the Mausoleum.

Historical Apartments

The Historical Apartments have been restored to their original form and decoration, with tapestries, silk damasks, panelling, mirrors and ceiling-paintings.

At the W end of the central range are the apartments occupied by Frederick I (bedroom, study, Red Braid Room, audience chamber) and his second wife Sophie Charlotte (audience chamber, antechamber, living apartments), with Chinese lacquer furniture or European imitations and inlaid and carved furniture of about 1700. The pictures are by Pesne, Schoojans,

Opening times
Tue.–Sun. 9 a.m.–5 p.m.

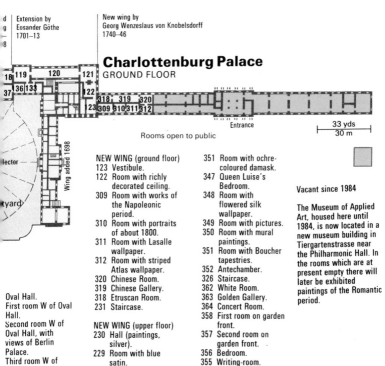

Extension by
Eosander Göthe
1701–13

New wing by
Georg Wenzeslaus von Knobelsdorff
1740–46

Charlottenburg Palace
GROUND FLOOR

Entrance

Rooms open to public

33 yds
30 m

Wing added 1698

Oval Hall.
First room W of Oval Hall.
Second room W of Oval Hall, with views of Berlin Palace.
Third room W of Oval Hall.

NEW WING (ground floor)
123 Vestibule.
122 Room with richly decorated ceiling.
309 Room with works of the Napoleonic period.
310 Room with portraits of about 1800.
311 Room with Lasalle wallpaper.
312 Room with striped Atlas wallpaper.
320 Chinese Room.
319 Chinese Gallery.
318 Etruscan Room.
231 Staircase.

NEW WING (upper floor)
230 Hall (paintings, silver).
229 Room with blue satin.
228 Room painted light blue.

351 Room with ochre-coloured damask.
347 Queen Luise's Bedroom.
348 Room with flowered silk wallpaper.
349 Room with pictures.
350 Room with mural paintings.
351 Room with Boucher tapestries.
352 Antechamber.
326 Staircase.
362 White Room.
363 Golden Gallery.
364 Concert Room.
358 First room on garden front.
357 Second room on garden front.
356 Bedroom.
355 Writing-room.
354 Library.
353 Silver Room.

Vacant since 1984

The Museum of Applied Art, housed here until 1984, is now located in a new museum building in Tiergartenstrasse near the Philharmonic Hall. In the rooms which are at present empty there will later be exhibited paintings of the Romantic period.

Charlottenburg Palace

Golden Gallery, Charlottenburg

Weidemann and other artists; the tapestries are from the Berlin manufactory of Charles Vigne.

The Porcelain Cabinet contains East Asian porcelain of the 17th and 18th c. The Palace Chapel, in which King Frederick William II was married morganatically to Countess Julie von Ingenheim in 1787, has been completely rebuilt.

At the E end of the central range, on the ground floor, are the Oak Gallery, in which concerts of chamber music are given from time to time.

On the ground floor of the New Wing, built by Georg Wenzeslaus von Knobelsdorff in the reign of Frederick the Great, are the apartments where Frederick William II passed the summers from 1788 and also the quarters of Frederick William III. Their décor, furniture, paintings and porcelain date from the Biedermeier period.

On the first floor of this wing are situated the apartments of Frederick the Great and the two principal State Reception Rooms of the palace.

Both reception rooms were originally furnished in pure Rococo style by Georg Wenzeslaus von Knobelsdorff and Nahl. They were destroyed in the Second World War but have been partially restored in their original form. The walls of the State Dining Room are covered with pink stucco in imitation of marble; the Golden Gallery on the east occupies the whole width of the wing and has imaginative gilded stucco decoration.

The former living quarters of Frederick the Great can also be visited. In the library can be seen bookcases, many souvenirs of Sanssouci Palace, and in the second apartment behind the

The Knobelsdorff Wing (New Wing) of the Palace

Golden Gallery a notable collection of paintings, especially works by Watteau, including his "Embarkation for Cythera", as well as other works of the French school from the beginning of the 18th c.

Museum of Prehistory

The Museum of Prehistory is housed in the Langhans Wing (West Wing), in what was originally the palace theatre. Although much important material (including Schliemann's finds from Troy) was lost during the Second World War, the collection has been supplemented by new acquisitions and excavation material and presents an excellent survey of the prehistory of Europe and the East.

Ground floor
Room 1: Material (originals or reproductions) of the hunting, gathering and fishing cultures of the Palaeolithic and Mesolithic (to 5000 B.C.).
Room 2: Farming cultures of the Neolithic (to 2000 B.C.) and material from western Asia.

Upper floor
Room 3: Bronze and Iron Age material, and prehistoric material from Brandenburg and the Berlin area (including the tomb chamber of a royal tomb at Seddin and a gold hoard from Eberswalde).

Opening times
Mon.–Thu., Sat. and Sun.
9–a.m.–5 p.m.

Closed
Fri.; 1 May

Charlottenburg Palace

Grand Courtyard and Park

Statue of the Great Elector

The equestrian statue of the Great Elector, Frederick William of Brandenburg, is one of the finest such statues of the Baroque period. Frederick William's son, Elector Frederick III, commissioned this monumental piece of sculpture from Andreas Schlüter to honour his father as founder of the State of Brandenburg and Prussia. The casting of the statue began in October 1700, and the monument was ceremonially unveiled on 12 July 1703, the Elector's birthday.

The Great Elector is represented partly in Roman and partly in contemporary garb, with a bronze breastplate and a flowing full-bottomed wig, holding out his baton in a commanding gesture. On the marble base is a finely modelled shield with a Latin inscription dedicated by the son to his father. At each end of the base are fettered slaves, symbolising the enemies overcome by the Great Elector.

The statue originally stood on the Long Bridge (Elector's Bridge), and later in front of the Town Palace. In 1943 it was removed for safety, but the boat which was transporting it was overloaded and sank in Tegel Harbour. The statue was recovered in 1949, and three years later was set up in the courtyard of Charlottenburg.

Park

The park – one of the most popular of Berlin's parks – was laid out in the French style in 1697 by Siméon Godeau, but in the early 19th c. much of it was remodelled by Peter Joseph Lenné as an English-style landscaped park. After the Second World War the central section was restored to its original Baroque form.

On the garden front of the palace are 24 marble busts of Roman emperors and empresses.

Schinkel Pavilion

Opening times
Tue.–Sun. 9 a.m.–5 p.m.

The Schinkel Pavilion (or New Pavilion) at the E entrance to the park was built by Karl Friedrich Schinkel in 1788 in the style of a Neapolitan villa for Frederick William III and his second wife Princess Liegnitz. The pavilion contains paintings by Caspar David Friedrich, the leading member of the German Romantic school, and other artists, together with furniture and pictures of the late 18th c.

Belvedere

Opening times
Tue.–Sun. 9 a.m.–5 p.m.

In the northern part of the park is the Belvedere, built by Carl Gotthard Langhans as a tea-house, which now contains a collection of Berlin porcelain (see National Porcelain Manufactory) of the 18th and early 19th c.

Mausoleum

Opening times
Apr.–Oct., Tue.–Sun.
10 a.m.–5 p.m.

On the west side of the park, at the end of an avenue of firs, stands a small Doric temple with columns of Brandenburg granite. This is the Mausoleum built by Heinrich Gentz for Frederick William III as the last resting-place of Queen Luise; it was completed in 1812.

The Mausoleum stands in a clump of trees, with a flight of eight steps leading up to a chamber with four Doric columns, containing the sarcophagus and a statue of Queen Luise, both by Christian Daniel Rauch. The Queen is represented sleeping, draped in a loose garment, with folded hands.

Thirty years later her husband was buried here, in a sarcophagus which was also the work of Rauch. His statue depicts him in a plain military cloak.

Later burials here include Prince Albert (1837–1906), the

Emperor William I (1797–1888) and his wife the Empress Augusta (1811–90), and Princess Liegnitz, second wife of Frederick William III (1800–73). The heart of Frederick William IV (eldest son of King Frederick William III, 1795–1861) is contained in a stone casket.

Congress Hall (Kongresshalle) B4

The Congress Hall was built as the American contribution to the International Building Exhibition of 1957 (see Hansaviertel).

The roof of the hall, rising to a height of 18 m (60 ft), resembled an open oyster-shell, and was at once christened the "Pregnant Oyster" by irreverent Berliners.

In the summer of 1980, however, much of the boldly conceived roof structure collapsed, and since then the Congress Hall has been closed. Rebuilding is planned for 1987.

Location
John-Foster-Dulles-Allee,
Tiergarten

Dahlem Church C3

This old village church, dedicated to St Anne, stands near Dahlem House (see next entry). The church, built of brick, dates from about 1220; the Late Gothic chancel is 15th c. The Baroque pulpit and gallery were added in 1679. There is a very fine carved wooden altar. From 1832 to 1892 the church tower was used as a relay station on the first optical telegraph line between Berlin and Koblenz.

The little church has now become a fashionable place for weddings and christenings.

Location
Königin-Luise-Strasse,
Dahlem

U-Bahn
Dahlem-Dorf

Buses
1, 10, 17

Dahlem House (Gutshaus Dahlem) C3

Nothing is known about the original foundation of Dahlem: the first evidence of occupation (potsherds) dates from the 13th c. The name appears in the form "Dalm" in Charles IV's Land Register of 1375, and is next mentioned in a tax register of 1450 as a fief held by Otto von Milow. In 1483 the property passed into the hands of the von Spil family, who lived there for 200 years. In 1665 it was sold for 3300 thalers to Georg Adam von Pfuhl; in 1671 it was acquired by the Willmerstorff family, and the settlement increased in size; and in 1679 the present mansion-house was built. Having withstood all the troubles of subsequent centuries, it now houses the Institute of Veterinary Medicine of the Free University of Berlin.

Location
Königin-Luise-Str. 49,
Dahlem

U-Bahn
Dahlem-Dorf

Buses
1, 10, 17, 60

**Dahlem Museums C3

The three-storey building with the massive portico which houses the Dahlem Museums was built by Bruno Paul between 1914 and 1923. Originally erected to accommodate the Asiatic Museum, it was subsequently enlarged on several occasions and now contains the Picture Gallery, the Print Cabinet, the

Location
Arnimallee 23–27,
Lansstrasse 8, Dahlem

U-Bahn
Dahlem-Dorf

Dahlem Museums

Museums of Indian, Islamic and East Asian Art, the Museum of Ethnography and the Sculpture Gallery.

About 1990 the Picture Gallery and the Print Cabinet are due to be transferred to the Prussian Cultural Heritage Foundation near the Philharmonic Hall (see entry).

Closed: Mon.; 1 Jan., 1 May, 24, 25 and 31 Dec.

Picture Gallery

Entrance
Arnimallee

The Picture Gallery, with a collection of European painting of all schools from the Middle Ages to the Neo-Classical period, is housed on the ground and upper floors.

The nucleus of the gallery was provided by the royal collections, considerably enlarged in the 20th c. In spite of heavy losses during the Second World War it still offers an excellent survey of European painting up to 1800.

German painting
Eight works by Dürer, including the "Virgin with the Goldfinch", the "Woman by the Sea" and the famous portraits of Hieronymus Holzschuher and Jacob Muffel; also works by Albrecht Altdorfer, Lucas Cranach and Hans Holbein the Younger.

Dutch and Flemish painting
Of particular importance are the Rembrandts, including the "Man with a Golden Helmet". There are also well-known works by Hieronymus Bosch, Brueghel, Van Cleve, Van Dyck, Van Eyck, Hugo van der Goes, Lucas van Leyden, Hans Memling, Rubens and Rogier van der Weyden.

Italian painting
Notable among works by Italian masters are paintings by Botticelli, Giotto, Filippo Lippi and Raphael.

French painting
Three works by Poussin, a landscape by Claude Lorrain and pictures by Georges de la Tour and the Le Nain brothers (17th c.); also works by 18th c. artists including Watteau, Antoine Pesne and Jean Restout.

Spanish painting
El Greco's "Mater Dolorosa" and pictures by Goya, Velázquez and Zurbarán.

Sculpture Gallery

Entrance
Arnimallee

The collection, displayed on the ground and upper floors, contains masterpieces of Western art from the Early Christian and Byzantine periods to the end of the 18th c. It includes icons, goldsmith's work, bronzes, ivories and woodcarving of the 3rd–7th c., Italian and Spanish sculpture (Bernini, Donatello, Luca della Robbia, Rossellino, Sansovino, etc.) and works by Multscher, Riemenschneider and other German sculptors.

Dahlem Museums

UPPER FLOOR

GROUND FLOOR

Entrance (Arnimallee)

Entrance (Lansstrasse)

LOWER FLOOR

TOP FLOOR
(not shown on plan)
13 Print Cabinet
14 Museum of Ethnography (East Asia)

UPPER FLOOR
3 Museum of Ethnography (South Seas)
4 Sculpture Gallery
5 Picture Gallery
7 Museum of Ethnography (Africa)
9 Museum of Islamic Art
10 Museum of East Asian Art
11 Museum of Ethnography (Southern Asia)
12 Special exhibitions

GROUND FLOOR
1 Museum of Indian Art
2 Museum of Ethnography (America)
3 Museum of Ethnography (South Seas)
4 Sculpture Gallery
5 Picture Gallery

LOWER FLOOR
A Lecture Room
B Young People's Museum
C Cafeteria
D Museum for the Blind

41

The Dahlem Museums

Museum of Indian Art

Entrance
Lansstrasse

The Museum of Indian Art displays a unique range of material and should on no account be omitted in a visit to the Dahlem Museums. It is devoted to the art of India, South-East Asia, Indonesia and Central Asia and includes, among much else, bronzes, woodcarving, painting, sculpture in stone, applied arts, frescoes from Turfan and early Sanskrit manuscripts.

Museum of Islamic Art

Entrance
Lansstrasse

The Museum of Islamic Art, housed on the upper floor, contains sculpture and applied art from the beginning of the Islamic period (8th c.) to the 18th c., covering not only the Muslim countries of the East but also India and Spain.
The exhibits include metalwork, ivories, pottery, glass, knotted carpets, miniatures, fabrics, small items of furniture, books and manuscripts.

Museum of East Asian Art

Entrance
Lansstrasse

The collection covers the art of China, Korea and Japan from the 2nd c. to the present day, including bronzes, pottery and porcelain, painting, woodcuts, sculpture, lacquerwork, jade, grave furnishings and small sculptures.

Queen Nefertiti (Egyptian Museum) ▶

Museum of Ethnography

Entrance
Lansstrasse

This museum takes a leading place among the ethnographic museums of Europe. Owing to shortage of space it can exhibit only a proportion of its holdings, though what is on show is excellently presented.

The museum possesses a total of almost half a million items from all parts of the world, covering ancient America (ground floor), the South Seas (ground and upper floors), Africa (upper floor) and Asia (upper and top floors). Of particular interest are the Ife terracotta sculpture, the Benin bronzes, the Peruvian pottery, the Boat Hall and the hall displaying native huts from New Guinea and New Zealand.

Print Cabinet

Entrance
Arnimallee

The collection includes printed graphic art, woodcuts and engravings of all European schools of the 15th–18th c., drawings (mainly 15th and 16th c. German masters), illustrated books, incunabula, miniatures and heraldic records.

Items not on display can be seen in the study room. The Print Cabinet also has an extensive photographic archive, including photographs of items in other galleries and collections.

Egyptian Museum (Ägyptisches Museum)   B3

Location
Schlossstrasse 70,
Charlottenburg

U-Bahn
Richard-Wagner-Platz

Buses
21, 54, 62, 74

Opening times
Mon.–Thu., Sat. and Sun.
9 a.m.–5 p.m.

Closed
Fri.; 1 May

The Egyptian Museum has been housed since 1967 in the eastern part of the Neo-Classical Stülerbau (Stüler Building), erected by Friedrich August Stüler in 1850, which lies opposite Charlottenburg Palace. Its 17 rooms display a wide range of material illustrating the art and culture of ancient Egypt from 5000 B.C. to A.D. 300.

The most celebrated exhibits are the limestone head of Queen Nefertiti, the ebony head of Queen Tiy, the funerary stela of a royal sculptor named Bak and his wife, the head of a priest in green stone and the Kalabsha Gate, presented to the Federal Republic by the Egyptian Government in gratitude for German financial and technical help in rescuing archaeological treasures endangered by the construction of the Aswan High Dam.

Apart from these outstanding items, however, there is much else of interest in the Egyptian Museum – pottery, statues, reliefs, tomb furnishings, stucco mummy masks, papyrus rolls, etc.

Emperor Frederick Memorial Church   B4 (a IV)
(Kaiser-Friedrich-Gedächtniskirche)

Location
Hansaviertel, Tiergarten

S-Bahn
Tiergarten

This Protestant church is the only building in the Hansaviertel (see entry) which has been rebuilt on its original site. The old Neo-Gothic church, erected in 1892–95, was destroyed during the Second World War and was replaced by a new building, designed by Ludwig Lemmer, which was completed in 1957.

Emperor William Memorial Church ▶

Buses
16, 23

The stained glass is by Ludwig Peter Kowalski and other artists, the outer doors of cast aluminium by Gerhard Marcks, the fine modern organ (5100 pipes, 63 stops) by Karl Schuke.
The tower, with a free-hanging bell, is 68 m (223 ft) high and completely transparent.

*Emperor William Memorial Church   B/C4 (a IV)
(Kaiser-Wilhelm-Gedächtniskirche)

Location
Breitscheidplatz,
Charlottenburg

U- and S-Bahn
Zoologischer Garten

Buses
9, 19, 29, 54, 60, 69, 73, 90, 94

Adjoining the modern church (by Egon Eiermann, 1959–61) stands the ruined tower of the old Kaiser-Wilhelm-Gedächtniskirche, built in 1891–95 (architect Franz Schwechten) in honour of the Emperor William I, which was destroyed in an air attack on 23 November 1943. Years after the war the question arose of demolishing the stump of the tower and building a completely new church. But the Berliners wanted to retain their old church, or at any rate what remained of it; and accordingly Egon Eiermann incorporated the ruined tower in the new complex he designed, consisting of a blue-glazed octagon and a hexagonal tower. The Memorial Church has thus become a major Berlin landmark and a war memorial at the same time.
In recent years the tower has become increasingly fragile and in danger of collapse. It is at present stable, but it is not certain how long it will remain so. The necessary funds (estimated at 1½ million marks) for the restoration of this ruin in the heart of Berlin are, however, now available; and in the meantime the new part of the church has been renovated.

*Ernst-Reuter-Platz   B4 (a III)

Location
Charlottenburg

U-Bahn
Ernst-Reuter-Platz

Buses
54, 90

After the sudden death of Ernst Reuter, the popular Chief Burgomaster (Mayor) of Berlin, in 1953 one of the largest squares in the centre of the city was named after him. Reuter was elected as Senior Burgomaster in 1947 but was prevented by a Soviet veto from taking up office until the following year; he led the resistance to the Soviet blockade of Berlin in 1948–49, and became Chief Burgomaster in 1950.
The Ernst-Reuter-Platz, situated at the junction of five major streets (Hardenbergstrasse, Bismarckstrasse, Strasse des 17. Juni, Otto-Suhr-Allee, Marchstrasse), is one of the largest squares in Europe, measuring 130 m (140 yds) by 117 m (130 yds). In the centre of the square, surrounded by lawns, are two large basins with fountains which are illuminated after dark (from spring to autumn). The highest fountain sends a jet 23 m (75 ft) into the air; when there is a strong wind the height is automatically reduced.
On the north side of the square, in front of the Faculty of Architecture of the University of Technology, is a bronze sculpture by Bernhard Heiliger, "The Flame", set up here in 1963, on the tenth anniversary of Ernst Reuter's death.
Round the square are a series of modern buildings occupied by well-known firms and by institutes of the University of Technology.

Ernst-Reuter-Platz

Europa-Center   C4

The Europa-Center, a 22-storey tower block 68 m (282 ft)
high, was built in 1963–65 to the design of K. H. Pepper, and
became popularly known to Berliners as "Pepper's Manhat-
tan". Within this huge shopping centre – area 90,000 sq. m
(98,460 sq. yd) – are about 100 shops, boutiques and
restaurants, a hotel, five first-run cinemas, a multivisions show,
the "Stachelschweine" (porcupines) cabaret, the revue theatre
"La vie en rose", galleries, a water-clock, service shops, the
"i-Punkt" Restaurant and café dansant (observation platform
with a magnificent view of the city), the Berlin Casino (open
daily 3 p.m.–3 a.m.) and the Tourist Information Office.
In Breitscheidplatz stands a large spherical fountain (1983)
known locally as "Wasserklops" (meatball).

Location
Breitscheidplatz

U- and S-Bahn
Zoologischer Garten

Buses
9, 19, 29, 60, 69, 73

Federal House (Bundeshaus Berlin)   C4

The building now known as the "Bundeshaus" was originally
erected in 1893–95 as an artillery depot which was closed
down after the First World War. Thereafter it was occupied
successively by the Reichswehr, a National Socialist unit, the
Soviet Army and the German Railways, and then for a time
stood empty.
With the establishment of the Federal Government in Bonn, the
question arose of how Berlin should participate in the political

Location
Bundesallee 216–218,
Wilmersdorf

U-Bahn
Spichernstrasse

Bus
69

47

life of the Federal Republic. For this purpose the post of Federal Representative in Berlin was established, and the old military buildings, renamed the Bundeshaus (Federal House), were brought back into use to house his office and the branch offices of various Federal Ministries. The first Federal Representative, appointed by the Federal Chancellor in 1950, was Heinrich Vockel, who was succeeded by Felix von Eckardt, Carl Krautwig, Egon Bahr, Dietrich Spangenberg and Hans-Jurgen Wischnewski; since 1983 it has been the Parliamentary Secretary of State Peter Lorenz.

Free University of Berlin (Freie Universität Berlin) C3

After the division of Berlin its University (the Humboldt University) lay in the Eastern half of the city. Accordingly in December 1948 a new Free University of Berlin was established in the American Sector, with the approval of the US Governor, General Lucius D. Clay, on the initiative of a "founding committee" headed by the Burgomaster, Ernst Reuter.
When it opened in 1948 the Free University had three faculties. The first major expansion came in 1952, with funds provided by the Ford Foundation (Henry Ford Building). In 1954 the University Library was opened. Then, four months after the death of Ernst Reuter, then Chief Burgomaster of Berlin, the Ernst Reuter Society of Patrons and Friends of the Free University was established to provide funds for further development. Thanks to a grant from the US State Department the first student vilage was built in Schlachtensee, and a further American contribution led to the foundation in 1963 of the American Institute (John F. Kennedy Institute), which moved into its new premises in 1967. When President John F. Kennedy visited Berlin in 1963 he was given an Honorary Doctorate of the Free University.
In accordance with the regulations of the Province of Berlin applying to universities, the Free University has since 1969 had a new constitution with a president. Today there are more than 50,000 students at the university.

Location
Garystrasse,
Zehlendorf, Dahlem

U-Bahn
Thielplatz

Buses
1, 11

* Glienicke Palace (Schloss Glienicke: officially Kleinglienicke) D1

Schloss Glienicke, originally a small country house, was built in its present form in 1826 by Karl Friedrich Schinkel as a summer residence for Prince Carl of Prussia. Neo-Classical in style, it consists of a main block with two side wings enclosing an Italian-style courtyard with a fountain. Built into the walls of the courtyard are numerous ancient fragments and inscriptions brought back by Prince Carl from his travels.

Location
Königinstrasse, Zehlendorf

Bus
6

The Glienicke Bridge, with sandstone piers and approaches, spans two small lakes, the Jungfernsee and Tiefer See. Built in 1908–09, it now lies on the boundary between West Berlin and Potsdam in East Germany; the crossing is used by the Allied occupation authorities. The bridge has been renamed Brücke

Glienicke Bridge (Glienicker Brücke)

◀ *In the Europa-Center*

Gropiusstadt

Gropiusstadt

der Einheit (Unity Bridge) by the German Democratic Republic.

Kleinglienicke Park
(Volkspark Kleinglienicke)

The park of Schloss Glienicke (area 116 hectares (287 acres)), opened to the public in 1934, lies close to the Peacock Island (Pfaueninsel: see entry) on the boundary between West Berlin and the German Democratic Republic.

The park was laid out by Peter Joseph Lenné from 1816 onwards. The owner at that time was Prince Hardenberg, but in 1824 the palace and park were acquired by Prince Carl of Prussia. The park affords fine views of the Havel and Potsdam (see entries), and has a beautiful riverside and lakeside walk running from the Glienicke Bridge to the Pfaueninsel (which was also laid out by Lenné).

The Nikolskoe viewpoint was also the work of Lenné. Here Frederick William III had a log cabin built for his daughter in 1819, naming it Nikolskoe in honour of his son-in-law Tsar Nicholas of Russia. The Church of SS. Peter and Paul, with its Russian-style onion dome, was built here by F. A. Stüler and J. G. Schadow in 1834–37; it is still used for worship.

Gropiusstadt (Gropius City)   C5/6

Location
Neukölln

This huge residential development, begun in 1962 in what was then open country in the districts of Rudow and Buckow (Neukölln), now totals some 18,250 dwellings. The general plan was the work of Walter Gropius (d. 1969), founder of the

Bauhaus in Weimar; the architects for the various sections of the development were selected by competition.

The area became popularly known as Gropiusstadt (Gropius City), and in 1972 this name was given official sanction.

The development includes detached houses, low blocks of flats and many tower blocks, the tallest of which is some 90 m (295 ft) high, with 31 floors. It also includes many shopping centres, public baths, a comprehensive school, a crêche, facilities for senior citizens, sports grounds and its own power-station for providing central heating.

U-Bahn
Johannisthaler Chaussee,
Lipschitzallee

Buses
41, 52

---

*Grunewald

C2/3

This area of forest of 32 sq. km (12⅓ sq. miles) lies E of the Havel between Heerstrasse and the Wannsee. The name is derived from a hunting-lodge built here in 1542 by Elector Joachim II and named Zum grünen Wald (Greenwood). The name of Grunewald came into use only in the 19th c.: the earlier name was Spandau Forest (Spandauer Forst).

The natural mixed forest of oak and beech has increasingly given place over the last 200 years or so to quickly growing species such as pine and birch, acacia and poplar. In recent years, however, planting has been designed to restore the original pattern.

During the severe winters after the last war and during the Soviet blockade (1948) 70 per cent of the trees were felled by freezing Berliners, who had no other form of fuel for heating. Since then the woods have been completely replanted, and now house a wide range of birds and other wildlife, including fallow deer, roe deer, wild pigs (in the Saubucht) and moufflons.

The Grunewald is traversed by an Ice Age melt-water channel with patches of bog and fen and three little lakes, the Pechsee, Barssee and Teufelssee.

The total area of the nature reserves, containing rare species of plants and animals (Langes Luch, Riemeisterfenn), is 111 hectares (274 acres).

The Grunewald, originally a royal hunting reserve, was opened to the public only at the end of the 19th c. In 1915 it was acquired by the city.

Numerous lakes in the eastern part of the Grunewald (Hundekehlesee, Grunewaldsee, Schlachtensee, Krumme Lanke) and 9 km (5½ miles) of riverbank along the Havel in the W offer facilities for bathing. Other popular features are the Teufelsberg (see entry), the Grunewald Tower, the Schildhorn and Grunewald Hunting-Lodge (see entry).

Location
Wilmersdorf/Zehlendorf

S-Bahn
Grunewald

The red-brick Grunewald Tower, formerly known as the Emperor William Tower, was erected in 1897–98 to commemorate William I. It contains a marble statue of the Emperor.

From the top of the tower (56 m (184 ft)) there are fine views of the forest, extending far into the German Democratic Republic.

Grunewald Tower
(Grunewaldturm)

In summer there are excursion coaches to the Grunewald from the Zoo Station, Hardenbergplatz. The steamer landing-stage is on the banks of the Havel below the Grunewald Tower. Near by is a garden restaurant with a fine view of the Havel.

Hunt on St Hubert's Day in the Grunewald

Grunewald Hunting-Lodge

*Grunewald Hunting-Lodge (Jagdschloss Grunewald: Museum)   C3

From the Königin Luise Strasse bus stop it is a 20 minutes' walk through the Grunewald to this hunting-lodge on the Grunewaldsee, built by Caspar Theyss for the Elector Joachim II of Brandenburg in 1542. Originally a plain Renaissance-style building, it was frequently altered in later periods. In 1593, during the reign of the Elector John George, an oriel window was added to the rear façade; under King Frederick I of Prussia (1657–1713) the house was completely renovated and much altered; and finally the service courtyard and store-rooms for hunting equipment were added in the reign of Frederick the Great (1712–86). Frederick William II (1744–97) reintroduced the traditional Red Hunt on St Hubert's Day (3 November) – a tradition still maintained by the Berlin riding clubs.

The house was the scene of great activity in 1814, when the Quadriga from the Brandenburg Gate (see entry), which Napoleon had carried off to France, was brought back to Berlin and stored here before being returned to its original position.

In 1949 the house was reopened as a museum, and in 1963 it was restored to its original form and colour. The collection of pictures of the 15th–19th c. includes rare works by Barthel Bryn, Lucas Cranach, Anton Graff, van Haarlem, Jacob Jordaens, Franz Krüger, Antoine Pesne and other artists.

The old store-rooms now house a small Hunting Museum, opened in 1970, with a collection of hunting equipment and trophies.

Location
Grunewald

Buses
10, 17, 60

Opening times
Tue.–Sun. 10 a.m.–5 p.m.,

Hunting Museum
(Jagdmuseum)

In the Hansaviertel

Hahn-Meitner Institute of Nuclear Research   D1
(Institut für Kernforschung)

Location
Glienicker Strasse,
Zehlendorf (Wannsee)

Bus
18

The Institute of Nuclear Research, founded in 1956, is named after Otto Hahn and Luise Meitner, who first achieved nuclear fission. It is concerned principally with fundamental research, and is one of the major research institutions supported by Federal funds.

The Institute is divided into four sections (nuclear and radiation physics, radiation chemistry, nuclear chemistry and reactors, data processing and electronics). Among its major research facilities is the BER II research reactor, with an output of 5 MW.

Hansaviertel (Hanseatic Quarter)   B4 (a IV)

Location
Tiergarten

U-Bahn
Hansplatz

S-Bahn
Bellevue, Tiergarten

Buses
16, 23, 24, 69

In the 19th c. this area near the Tiergarten was a residential district much favoured by the prosperous middle classes, with houses of the traditional Berlin type (a front wing on the street, with two side wings linked by a range to the rear). The old quarter was almost completely destroyed during the Second World War, and in 1953 the Berlin Senate resolved that it should be rebuilt, but with a more open layout.

The project was carried out as a collaborative effort by 48 leading architects from many different countries. Work began in 1955, and in 1957 the scheme was the central feature of the International Building Exhibition held in Berlin. The complex comprises detached houses and blocks of flats, a congress hall, a school and a crèche, Protestant and Roman Catholic

▼   *Landscape on the Havel*

churches, a library, a cinema and shops. The ten landscape-architects who were involved in the project contrived to extend the landscape of the Tiergarten – which had also been replanted – well into the housing area. In consequence the Hansaviertel has now once again the air of a settled community.

*Hasenheide Park (Volkspark Hasenheide)   C5

Hasenheide Park covering an area of 56 hectares (138 acres) and situated in a densely populated part of the city, was laid out by Peter Joseph Lenné in 1838. From 1878 it was used as a shooting-range by the Berlin garrison, and it became a public park only in 1936–39. After the Second World War it was extended to take in the Rixdorfer Höhe, a hill formed of rubble from buildings destroyed during the war. A nature trail was laid out, and a variety of facilities for recreation and relaxation were provided – wide expanses of grass, children's playgrounds, enclosures in which animals could range at liberty, heath and rhododendron gardens and an open-air theatre.

To Berliners the Hasenheide is associated with the name of "Turnvater" Jahn – Friedrich Ludwig Jahn, who opened the first gymnasium in Germany here in 1810 with the idea of toughening the youth of Prussia by a Spartan way of life and the practice of gymnastics. But his outspoken political opinions displeased the authorities: he was arrested, his gymnasium was closed in 1819 and the practice of gymnastics was prohibited. There is now a monument to Jahn (by Erdmann Encke, 1872) in the park.

There is another monument in the park commemorating a very

Location
Columbiadamm, Neukölln

U-Bahn
Hermannplatz

Buses
4, 28, 91

different historical situation. Erected in 1955 on the Rixdorfer Höhe, this monument (by Katharina Singer) honours the "Trümmerfrauen", the "rubble women" who played their part in the rebuilding of Berlin after the war.

*Havel, River

A–C2

The River Havel flows through Berlin for 30 km (19 miles) of its total length of 340 km (210 miles). It rises near Neustrelitz in Mecklenburg, traverses Berlin from N to S and finally joins the Elbe at Ruhstädt-Gnevsdorf, near Havelberg. It is linked by canals with other natural watercourses, and its principal tributary is the Spree, which flows into the Havel at Spandau. The level of the river within Berlin is regulated by sluices, but it can still occasionally flood. The most beautiful stretches of the Havel within the city area are around Schildhorn, Lindwerder, Schwanenwerder and the Pfaueninsel (see entry). On the left bank extends the Grunewald. The Havel lakes offer excellent facilities for a variety of water sports.

Havelchaussee

One good way of getting a general impression of the scenery of the Havel is a drive along the Havelchaussee. This road (maximum speed 30 km p.h. (19 m.p.h.)) starts from Teltower Strasse in Spandau and runs S past Tiefwerder, passes under Heerstrasse to enter the Grunewald and at Schildhorn circles round the Dachsberg before climbing to the Grunewald Tower, and then descends to the level of the river in a straight and relatively gradual descent. At the Lieper Bucht (bathing; feeding of swans in winter) the road follows the river to

▼ *The International Congress Centre*

the Grosse Steinlanke (bathing beach) and then, beyond a car park, climbs again on to an Ice Age dune. After some 2 km (1¼ miles) it joins Kronprinzessinnenweg, from which (turning right) it is a few minutes' drive to the Nikolassee district.

Another way of getting to know the landscape of the Havel is to take a boat trip on the river. In summer some 50 vessels belonging to private firms and the State-owned Stern- und Kreisschiffahrt ply on the Havel, the Spree and the canals; timetables are displayed at the ticket offices on the landing-stages. One good plan is to start from the Freybrücke landing-stage in Heerstrasse (Picheldorf, in Spandau) and take a boat which sails downstream past Schildhorn, the Grunewald Tower, the Hohengatow lido, Lindwerder and Breitehorn to Kladow; then take another boat and continue to the Pfaueninsel, the Wannsee and the Glienicke Bridge (see entries for Pfaueninsel, Wannsee and Glienicke Palace). From the Wannsee a BVG (municipal) bus or the S-Bahn can be taken back to the city centre.

A boat trip on the Havel

Passenger shipping traffic within the Berlin area has a long tradition which can be traced back to the year 1702. In those days there was a twice-daily service of boats, pulled by horses on a towpath alongside the Spree, between Berlin and Charlottenburg. The first steam-driven vessel in continental Europe was the "Prinzessin Charlotte von Preussen", 136 feet long, which was launched at Pichelsdorf on 14 August 1816. The latest novelty is the motor ship "Moby Dick" (built 1973), which is shaped externally in the form of a whale; it has a length of 48·3 m (158 ft) and a beam of 8·2 m (27 ft) and can carry 486 passengers.

Hunting Museum

See Grunewald Hunting-Lodge

*International Congress Centre C3
(Internationales Congress-Centrum: ICC)

Location
Messedamm 22,
Charlottenburg

U-Bahn
Kaiserdamm
(10 min. walk)

S-Bahn
Westkreuz
(10 min. walk)

Buses
4, 10, 65, 69, 94

The International Congress Centre lies between the Messedamm, a wide urban expressway, and the S-Bahn (suburban railway). It can be reached direct by way of the Avus, and there is a parking garage for 650 cars. An U-Bahn station is planned. A three-level bridge over the Messedamm links the Congress Centre with the exhibition grounds at the foot of the Radio Tower (see entry).

The Congress Centre, built between 1970 and 1979, is Berlin's largest post-war building. It is 320 m (1050 ft) long, 80 m (260 ft) across and 40 m (130 ft) high; it has a cubic content of 800,000 cu. m (1,000,000 cu. yds); the total weight of steel in the roof is 8500 tons. The building has a multi-layered skin which totally excludes outside noise and absorbs vibrations from the road. It has eight halls and many conference rooms, all linked with one another by an information and direction system using colours, numbers and symbols.

The largest hall (No. 1, Auditorium) can seat up to 5000 people. It has a stage with the most modern technical refinements.

On the entrance boulevard are a post office, a bank, shops, a medical centre, etc. and the Pullman Restaurant.

The Berliners have now accepted this monster of technical achievement. During the first five years there were about 2000 congresses and almost 2 million participants and visitors were recorded.

Information desk in the entrance hall. Tel. 30 38–1.

Jewish Community House (Jüdisches Gemeindehaus) C4

Location
Fasanenstr. 79–80,
Charlottenburg

Buses
9, 19, 29

U-Bahn
Uhlandstrasse

The Jewish Community House was built in 1959 (architects Dieter Knoblauch and Hans Heise) to replace the Synagogue of 1912 which was burned down by the Nazis in 1938. In front of the new building are some surviving fragments of the old one, serving as a reminder of the crimes of the Nazi period.

In addition to the accommodation required for worship the building contains rooms for meetings, etc., a library and a restaurant. On a bare grey concrete wall is a memorial tablet with the star of David and an inscription in bronze characters. In the columned hall are inscribed the names of concentration camps and ghettos.

The Jewish Community in Berlin numbers about 7000.

Kleinglienicke Park

See Glienicke Palace

Jewish Community House

Kreuzberg

The Kreuzberg (Hill of the Cross; 66 m (217 ft)) lies to the S of the city, near Tempelhof Airport, enclosed by Kreuzbergstrasse, the Mehringdamm, Dudenstrasse and Katzbachstrasse. The area round the hill (16 hectares (40 acres)) was laid out by Hermann Mächtig at the end of the 19th c. as the Viktoria-Park. About 1300 the hill was still known as the "Tempelhofer Berg", and it was then owned by the Franciscans. Until 1740 vines were grown here. In 1821 a monument designed by K. F. Schinkel was erected on the hill to commemorate the Wars of Liberation of 1813–15; it was crowned by an iron cross, and accordingly the hill was thereafter known as the Kreuzberg. There is a waterfall, artificially constructed in 1893 on the model of the Zackenfall in the Riesengebirge.

In summer a picture market is held at the foot of the Kreuzberg, when young artists offer their work for sale.

The district of Kreuzberg is the smallest in West Berlin (*c.* 130,000 inhabitants), but it has the highest density of population and the greatest number of foreigners (*c.* 27,000 Turks). Today efforts are being made to maintain the structure of the population and the street pattern of the quarter, and to redevelop in such a way that as little as possible is destroyed. On the Fraenkelufer and at the Schlesischen Tor are two new buildings for the International Building Exhibition (IBA) which is planned for 1987; the architects are I. and H. Baller and A. S. Vieira respectively. The well-known Anhalter Station (built

Location
Kreuzberg

U-Bahn
Platz der Luftbrücke

Buses
4, 19, 28

1874–80) once stood at Askanischen Platz; now only part of the façade and the portico remain. Transport Museum (see entry – Practical Information).

**Kurfürstendamm   C3/4 (b II/III)

Location
Wilmersdorf and
Charlottenburg

U-Bahn
Kurfürstendamm

Buses
9, 19, 29

The Kurfürstendamm, known to the Berliners simply as the "Ku'damm", is West Berlin's best-known and most popular shopping street and promenade, though there are those who feel that it has lost its former attraction and flair. Its numerous cafés, restaurants and bars, its cinemas and theatres still attract large numbers of people in quest of entertainment or relaxation; on fine summer days the crowds of visitors begin to thin out only shortly before midnight, and it is after midnight before there is any marked lull in the traffic.

In the 16th c. this was the route followed by the Elector Joachim II when riding to his hunting-lodge of Grunewald: hence the name Kurfürstendamm (Elector's Causeway). It was only at the end of the 19th c., on the initiative of Bismarck and with the approval of the Emperor William I, that it was developed into a main road, 3·5 km (2 miles) long, leading to the Grunewald.

Almost half of the 245 or so buildings erected along the Kurfürstendamm at the end of the 19th c. were completely destroyed in 1945, and the rest suffered damage in greater or lesser degree.

Lübars

The Church of Maria Regina Martyrum

Lübars

A4

This old village built concentrically round a nucleus, was first mentioned in the records in 1247; it has preserved its rural character and is now a statutorily protected national monument. It lies on the northern edge of West Berlin, close to the frontier with the German Democratic Republic, surrounded by fields and meadows. In the past it was so well concealed that even the marauding soldiers of the Thirty Years War failed to discover it.

There is much good walking to be had in the surrounding area, for example on the footpaths between Tegel and Hermsdorf, running through the characteristic fenland of Brandenburg with its rich flora and fauna.

In winter the village is a pocket of cold, with the lowest temperatures in Berlin.

Lübars has a country-style village inn, from which the walker can continue on his way to the Valley of the Tegeler Fliess.

Location
Reinickendorf

Bus
20

* Maria Regina Martyrum, Church of

B3

The uncompromisingly rectangular and undecorated church of Mary Queen of the Martyrs, near the Plötzensee Memorial (see entry), was built in 1960–62 as a memorial to those who died between 1933 (Hitler's accession to power) and 1945. It consists of a lower church with three memorial tombs and the

Location
Heckerdamm 230–232,
Charlottenburg

Buses
9, 21, 23, 62

church proper above it. The whole of the chancel wall is occupied by a fresco of an apocalyptic vision by Georg Meistermann, and one wall of the courtyard has a series of abstract Stations of the Cross in bronze by Otto H. Hajek.

Mariendorf Church

C5

Location
Alt-Mariendorf

U-Bahn
Alt-Mariendorf

This little village church, built of granite in Late Romanesque style, dates from the beginning of the 13th c. The Baroque W tower, with a wooden superstructure and a curved copper roof (1737), contains a bell of 1480.

Marienfelde Church

D4

Location
Alt-Marienfelde

Buses
11, 30, 32, 52

The village church of Marienfelde is the oldest church in Berlin and one of the oldest in Brandenburg. Built of local stone and natural boulders, it was erected by the Templars about 1220 and taken over by the Order of St John in 1318. In 1435 it passed into the hands of the town councils of Berlin and Cölln. It was restored in 1921.

Märkisches Viertel (Brandenburg Quarter)

A4

Location
Reinickendorf (Wittenau)

S-Bahn
Wittenau (Nordbahn)

Buses
14, 21, 22, 62

Like Gropiusstadt (see entry), the Märkisches Viertel, the "Brandenburg Quarter" named after the Mark (March) Brandenburg, is a modern satellite town, built between 1964 and 1972 on an area of 280 hectares (690 acres) formerly occupied by allotments. This new settlement with its brightly painted high-rise blocks has a population of some 50,000. It has c. 20,300 houses and flats, 12 schools, 8 nursery schools and crêches, an old people's centre, a library, a swimming-pool, cinemas, community centres and a large shopping centre. The houses are grouped in neighbourhoods and surrounded by lawns and play areas.

But there is another aspect of the development which has made the Märkisches Viertel a social problem area. The flats are too small for the families occupying them, which tend to be large; there are inadequate recreation facilities and room for children to play; the areas of grass are lost amid the concrete. Originally there were none of the traditional bars beloved of the Berliners, and no community centres. The result was to produce a feeling of isolation, which often found vent in aggression. The Märkisches Viertel has thus become a classical example of well-intentioned planning that went wrong, a social project that has given rise to social problems.

The road to the picturesque village of Lübars (see entry) runs through the Märkisches Viertel.

*Museum of Antiquities (Antikenmuseum)

B3

The Museum of Antiquities has been housed since 1960 in the western part of the Cavalier building, designed by Friedrich

August Stüler (1800–65), the eastern part of which is occupied by the Egyptian Museum (see entry).

The nucleus of the collection came from the old Antiquarium, founded in 1830, which was dispersed during the Second World War and is now split between West Berlin and East Berlin (see Bode Museum, Early Christian-Byzantine collection).

On four floors are displayed notable examples of ancient art from the Minoan and Mycenaean periods to Early Byzantine times – Attic vases, Greek bronzes, jewellery and goldsmith's work, votive figures, mummy portraits, ivories.

The most celebrated exhibit is the Hildesheim Treasure, a hoard of silver vessels dating from the time of Augustus.

A new section, opened in 1984 on the second floor, has Etruscan, Roman and South Italian exhibits.

Location
Schlosstrasse 1,
Charlottenburg

U-Bahn
Richard-Wagner-Platz

Buses
54, 74, 87

Opening times
Mon.–Thu., Sat. and Sun.
9 a.m.–5 p.m.

Closed
Fri.; 1 May

Museum of Applied Art
(Kunstgewerbemuseum: National Museums of the Prussian Cultural Heritage)

The Museum of Applied Art, founded in 1867 and housed until 1984 in Charlottenburg Palace, has now been newly established in the "Cultural Forum". The collection includes examples from every field of European applied art from the Middle Ages to the 18th c.

On view are ceramics, porcelain, glass, Byzantine gold enamel ware, silver vessels, furniture, textiles and embroidery. Of special interest is the Guelf Treasure (gold and silver articles, both religious and profane from the House of Brunswick-Luneburg).

The museum also has Persian metalwork, articles from East Asia, Oriental carpets and exotic products.

Location
Tiergartenstrasse 6
Tiergarten

Buses
24, 48, 83

Opening times
Daily, except Mon. 9 a.m.–
5 p.m.

Museum of East Asian Art

See Dahlem Museums

Museum of Ethnography

See Dahlem Museums

Museum of Indian Art

See Dahlem Museums

Museum of Islamic Art

See Dahlem Museums

Museum of Islamic Art

National Library

Musical Instrument Museum, seen here when it was in the Bundesalle

Museum of Prehistory

See Charlottenburg Palace

*Musical Instrument Museum   C4

The Musical Instrument Museum, founded in 1888 is attached to the National Institute of Musical Research. Until the autumn of 1984 it was situated in the Bundesallee, but in the following December it was moved into premises in the "Cultural Forum" at the Philharmonic Hall.

The collection includes European and extra-European musical instruments from the 16th c. to the present day (among them valuable examples of the Renaissance and Baroque periods), as well as documentation (books, manuscripts, pictures) on the history of musical instruments.

The museum also has a reference library, an archive, a photographic collection and a large number of records and tapes of historic instruments.

Location
Tiergartenstrasse 1,
Tiergarten

Buses
24, 29, 48, 83

Opening times
Tue.–Sat. 9 a.m.–5 p.m.,
Sun. 10 a.m.–5 p.m.

Library
Tues.–Thurs. 10 a.m.–5 p.m.;
Fri. 10 a.m.–12 noon

National Archives (Geheimes Staatsarchiv)   C3

The National Archives contain a large collection of documents and records from the time of the Holy Roman Empire to the dissolution of the Prussian State, including the provincial archives of the March of Brandenburg, 50,000 historic maps and plans, a library of 80,000 volumes on the history of Prussia, and collections of charters, orders, coats of arms and seals from the German eastern territories.

There is a reading-room for students, but only very restricted lending facilities.

Location
Archivstrasse 12–14,
Zehlendorf (Dahlem)

U-Bahn
Dahlem-Dorf

Opening times
Reading room: Mon., Wed.,
Thu., Fri. 8 a.m.–3.30 p.m.;
Tue. 8 a.m.–7.30 p.m.

*National Library (Staatsbibliothek)   B4

The National Library is open to all, without charge.

The Library originated as the Prussian National Library, most of which was moved to western Germany during the last war; 1,700,000 volumes were stored in Marburg, and many manuscripts and prints found a temporary home in Tübingen University Library. All of these have now been returned to Berlin.

The new library – one of the largest and finest libraries built in Europe since the war – was erected in 1967–68; the architect was Hans Scharoun, who also designed the Philharmonic Hall (see entry). The site has an area of 38,000 sq. m (45,450 sq. yds), just over half of which is occupied by the library itself. The building measures 229 m (750 ft) by 152 m (500 ft) and has a total floor area of 81,300 sq. m (97,250 sq. yds).

A direction and information system beginning at the main entrance enables visitors to find their way about the building. The library has a capacity of 8 million volumes. Its present stock amounts to 3·5 million volumes from every field of knowledge and many countries.

Location
Potsdamer Strasse 33,
Tiergarten

U-Bahn
Kurfürstenstrasse
(then by bus)

Buses
24, 29, 48, 83

Opening times
Mon.-Fri. 9 a.m.–7 p.m., Sat.
9 a.m.–1 p.m.
Reading-room Mon.–Fri.
9 a.m.–9 p.m (holiday
periods only until 7 p.m.),
Sat. 9 a.m.–5 p.m.

Closed
Sun. and public holidays

National Porcelain Manufactory

National Porcelain Manufactory

Some 31,250 current newspapers and periodicals are kept and are available for consultation, as are 220,000 microfilms and microfiches.

Ibero-American Library

The projecting SW wing contains a specialised Ibero-American Library, a lecture hall seating 500 and a smaller hall with 100 seats.

Special departments

There are a Manuscript Department, a Music Department (with a collection of some 20,000 musical manuscripts), a special collection on the Mendelssohn family, a Map Department, an Eastern European Department, an Oriental Department (one of the world's largest collections of Oriental manuscripts) and an East Asian Department.

The Library's photographic archives contain some 5 million photographs of graphic art, prints, woodcuts, lithographs, etc.

National Porcelain Manufactory   B4 (a IV)

Location
Wegelystrasse 1, Tiergarten

S-Bahn
Tiergarten

It is a few minutes' walk from the bus stop or the S-Bahn to the National Porcelain Manufactory, an establishment with a tradition going back 250 years. Founded by Kaspar Wegely, it became the Royal Porcelain Manufactory (Königliche Porzellan-Manufaktur, KPM) in 1763, and Frederick the Great granted it the right to use the blue sceptre of Brandenburg as its

New National Gallery

trademark. Since then it has continued to produce both fine porcelain and ware for everyday use.

The manufactory has sale-rooms at Wegelystrasse 1 and Kurfürstendamm 205. A permanent exhibition of 500 pieces can be seen in the Belvedere of Charlottenburg Palace (see entry).

Bus
23

---

*New National Gallery (Neue Nationalgalerie)   B4

The National Gallery, a steel and glass structure designed by Ludwig Mies van der Rohe, was built in 1965–68. It consists of a square hall and a basement structure housing the collection. At the N and S ends flights of steps lead up to the platform on the roof of the basement structure, and the entrance is approached by another flight of steps on the main front.

The collection consists of pictures, sculpture and drawings of the 19th and 20th c., including the German Romantic school, the Realists, the German school in Rome, the French and German Impressionists, the Expressionists, the Bauhaus, the Surrealists and contemporary art. The gallery incorporates the old 19th Century Gallery in Jebenstrasse. It also puts on periodic special exhibitions.

Associated with the gallery are a workshop for the restoration of pictures and drawings, a reference library and a large collection of slides.

Location
Potsdamer Strasse 50,
Tiergarten

U-Bahn
Kurfürstenstrasse

Buses
24, 29, 48, 83

Opening times
Tue.–Sun. 9 a.m.–5 p.m.

Closed
Mon.; 1 Jan.

New National Gallery

The new Opera House

▼ *Olympic Stadium*

Observatory (Wilhelm-Foerster-Sternwarte)   C4

The Observatory bears the name of the Director of the old Berlin Observatory, beside the Zoo, which was destroyed during the last war. The new building stands on the Insulaner, a hill formed of rubble from demolished buildings; designed by Carl Bassen, it was built in 1962–63.
The Planetarium can show the night sky in any hemisphere, or as seen from space. There are lecture rooms, facilities for observing the sky and a dome with a Bamberg refractor.
There are regular lectures at 8 p.m. from Tuesday to Saturday and 5 p.m. on Sundays.

Location
Munsterdamm 90, on the Insulaner, Sterglitz

Buses
25, 68, 76, 83

Opening times
Telescope observation, Astronomical demonstrations: Tue., Thu., Fri., Sat. 6 p.m. and 9 p.m.; Sun. 3, 4, 5, 6 and 9 p.m.

*Olympic Stadium (Olympiastadion)   B3

The Olympic Stadium, designed by Werner March, was built in 1934–36 for the 1936 Summer Olympics. It replaced the German Stadium, built on the same site in 1913 by Otto March (Werner March's father).
The stadium can seat some 90,000 spectators, 30,000 of them under cover; the total length of the seating is about 41 km (25 miles). There are also a swimming stadium, a hockey stadium and a riding-track.
From the bell-tower (78 m (256 ft); express elevator) there are fine panoramic views of the stadium, the city and the River Havel, with distant prospects of Potsdam (see that entry) and

Location
Charlottenburg

U-Bahn
Olympiastadion

Bus
94

Opening times
Daily from 9 a.m. to dusk

the Müggelberge. The tower is open daily from April to October
between 10 a.m. and 5.30 p.m.
In the Murellen Hills to the west of the stadium is an open-air
theatre with 20,000 seats.

Closed
During sporting events

---

*Opera House (Deutsche Oper Berlin)   B4 (b III)

The Opera House, designed by Fritz Bornemann, was built in
1961 on the site of the old Municipal Opera House of 1912
which was destroyed during the last war. It incorporates some
surviving fragments of the earlier building.
A modern structure of steel and glass 70 m (230 ft) long, the
Opera House has a windowless façade of concrete slabs
designed to keep out street noise. In front of the building is a
piece of abstract steel sculpture by Hans Uhlmann, irreverently
referred to by the Berliners as the "Shashlik Spit".
The ticket office is open Mon.–Fri. 2–8 p.m., Sat., Sun. 10 a.m.–
2 p.m. and for an hour before performances.

Location
Bismarckstrasse 34–37

U-Bahn
Deutsche Oper

Bus
1

---

*Pfaueninsel (Peacock Island)   C1

The Pfaueninsel is a beautiful little island very typical of the
scenery of Brandenburg. This "Peacock Island", with an area of
98 hectares (242 acres), was once popularly known as
Kaninchenwerder (Rabbit Island). Boats are available from
Wannsee Station (return tickets) and a ferry service according
to demand from Haveluferweg.
At the end of the 17th c., in the time of the Great Elector,
Frederick William of Brandenburg, an alchemist named Johann
Kunckel had a glass factory on the island, the remains of which
have recently been excavated. After the death of his patron
Kunckel emigrated to Sweden in 1688.

Location
Zehlendorf

Buses
6, 18, to
Pfaueninselchaussee; special
buses from Zoo Station

In 1793 Frederick William II "rediscovered" the island and had
a half-timbered house built by a local craftsman for himself and
Wilhelmine Encke, later Countess Lichtenau – who is said to
have sketched out the design herself. Frederick William III and
his wife, Queen Luise, were fond of the house and used it as a
summer residence. It was during this period that the peacocks
from which the island takes its present name were introduced.
The castle is designed to look like a romantic ruin or folly, with
two towers linked by a footbridge (originally of wood), replaced
in 1807 by an iron bridge – an early product of the Berlin iron-
casting industry). The building was faced with concrete in
1909–11 and now houses a museum. The finely appointed
interior bears witness to the quality of the craftsmen of Berlin
and Potsdam. Particularly notable is the spiral staircase.

Castle

Opening times
Apr.–Sept., Tue.–Sun.
10 a.m.–4 p.m.

Closed
Oct.–Mar.

Originally covered with a luxuriant growth of natural vegetation, the island was laid out largely in the style of an English
landscaped park by Peter Joseph Lenné. It is now the home of
many rare plants. The menagerie established by Frederick
William III became the nucleus of the Berlin Zoo; the palm-
house designed by Schinkel was burned down at the end of the

Pfaueninsel Nature Reserve

◄ *Pfaueninsel: the Castle*

Philharmonic Hall

19th c.; and the rose-garden was transferred to Sanssouci. What remained was the vegetation, in particular the trees – Weymouth and Arolla pines, sequoias, ginkgos and cedars, as well as many native species. This is very pleasant walking country; cars are banned.

Scattered about amid the luxuriant vegetation are a number of houses and other buildings, including the memorial temple for Queen Luise, with a sandstone portico from the Mausoleum in the park of Charlottenburg Palace (1829), and the Kavaliershaus, designed by Schinkel, to which the façade of a Gothic patrician house in Danzig was built on in 1824–26. To the NE of the island is the Dairy Farm (Meierei), built, like the Castle, in the style of a mock ruin. Near by is the Schweizerhaus (Swiss Cottage), also designed by Schinkel (1830). An aviary built in 1834, set amid a dense growth of trees, is still in use.

All these various buildings are reached on winding footpaths laid out by Lenné. A walk round the island takes about 2 hours: before setting out it is wise to check the time of the last ferry.

*Philharmonic Hall (Philharmonie)   B4

Location
Mattäikirchstrasse 1,
Tiergarten

It was many years after the last war before Berlin acquired a worthy concert hall and the Berlin Philharmonic Orchestra gained a regular home. After the destruction of the old Philharmonic Hall the orchestra had found temporary quarters

Plötzensee Memorial

in the Academy of Music, but this accommodation had proved inadequate to their needs.

Buses
24, 29, 48, 83

The new Philharmonic Hall on the edge of the Tiergarten, designed by Hans Scharoun and built between 1960 and 1963, is an asymmetric structure with a tent-like concrete roof, whose exterior exactly reflects the functional design of the interior. The concert hall itself, with seating for 2000, is pentagonal in plan, with a central stage and the audience seated on terraces rising round it. This layout caused some surprise at first, since audiences were not used to the idea of looking at the backs of the orchestra, but it has now been accepted – largely, no doubt, because of the excellent acoustics in every part of the hall. Round the concert hall are a series of foyers linked with it by corridors.

Picture Gallery

See Dahlem Museums

Plötzensee Memorial (Gedenkstätte Plötzensee)   B4

After the Second World War Plötzensee became a symbol of the resistance to National Socialism, for within the walls of the prison here (now an institution for young offenders) some

Location
Hüttig-Pfad,
Charlottenburg-Nord

1800 people of different nations were executed for political reasons.

In 1952 the Berlin Senate resolved that the place of execution should become a memorial to the victims of Nazism. The memorial includes the execution shed, with the eight hooks in a roof beam on which these victims of Nazi justice were hanged – including no fewer than 89 who were involved in the attempt on Hitler's life on 20 July 1944.

In front of the shed are a memorial stone with the inscription "To the victims of the Hitler dictatorship of 1933–45" and a large stone urn containing earth from all the Nazi concentration camps.

Buses
23, 65, 89

Opening times
Daily 8.30 a.m.–5.30 p.m.

Print Cabinet

See Dahlem Museums

Radio Museum (Deutsches Rundfunkmuseum)　　　　C3

The Radio Museum, housed in an old studio at the foot of the Radio Tower (see entry), covers the development of radio transmission and reception from the beginning of broadcasting in Germany (1923) to the outbreak of the Second World War. It includes a faithful reproduction of the first German broadcasting studio of 1923.

The museum is open daily, except Tue. from 10 a.m. to 5 p.m.

Location
Hammarskjöldplatz 1,
Charlottenburg

Buses
4, 10, 65, 69, 94

---

*Radio Tower (Funkturm)　　　　C3 (a l)

The Radio Tower is one of Berlin's landmarks, ranking with the Brandenburg Gate and the Victory Column. Designed by Heinrich Straumer, it was begun in 1924 and began to operate in 1926, during the Third Radio Exhibition. The tower, looking like a miniature Eiffel Tower, has a total height of 138 m (453 ft). From the restaurant, situated at a height of 55 m (180 ft), and the observation platform at 126 m (413 ft; lift) there are magnificent panoramic views of the city.

At the foot of the tower are the Exhibition Grounds (Messegelände), with about 90,000 sq. m (98,640 sq. yd) of floor space in the 24 exhibition halls and 40,000 sq. m (48,000 sq. yd) of open ground.

Location
Exhibition Grounds
(Messegelände),
Charlottenburg

Buses
4, 10, 65, 69, 94

Opening times
Observation platform:
daily 10 a.m.–11.30 p.m.;
Restaurant:
daily 11 a.m.–9 p.m.

---

*Reichstag Building (Reichstagsgebäude)　　　　B4

With the proclamation of the German Empire in the Hall of Mirrors at Versailles on 18 January 1871 Berlin acquired a new role as capital of the Empire, and the Reichstag, the Imperial Parliament, needed a larger and more impressive building. The new Reichstag, a huge and regularly proportioned Neo-Renaissance palace, was designed by Paul Wallot; the

Location
Platz der Republik,
Tiergarten

S-Bahn
Lehrter Stadtbahnhof

◄　*Radio Tower*

Reichstag Building

Reichstag Building

Buses
69, 83

Opening times
Daily except Mon. 10 a.m.–
5 p.m.

foundation-stone was laid by the Emperor himself in 1884, and the building was completed in 1894. The cost (30 million marks) was met from French war reparations.

During the First World War the inscription "Dem deutschen Volke" ("To the German People") was carved on the pediment; it is still visible today.

On the evening of 27 February 1933, in circumstances which have never been fully elucidated, the Reichstag was destroyed by fire. The Nazi claim that the fire was started by members of the German Communist Party was refuted by the not-guilty verdict of the Supreme Court on the two Communists accused of the crime, Dimitrow and Torgler (December 1933). Nor has the Communist counter-claim that the Nazis themselves were responsible for the fire been proved. A Dutchman, Marinus van der Lubbe, was found guilty by the Supreme Court and condemned to death; in 1980 a German court dismissed the idea that he was solely responsible; and in 1981 this judgment was overturned, though on formal and not on substantial grounds. The question of responsibility for the fire, therefore, remains open.

The Reichstag fire was important not so much in itself as in its consequences; for it was the pretext for the emergency decree of 28 February 1933 which suspended the basic rights guaranteed by the Weimar Constitution and introduced the death penalty for a whole range of offences.

What was left of the Reichstag after the fire was destroyed in 1945 by bombing and looting. Rebuilding was completed in 1970, and visitors can now see an exhibition housed in the new

Reichstag Building

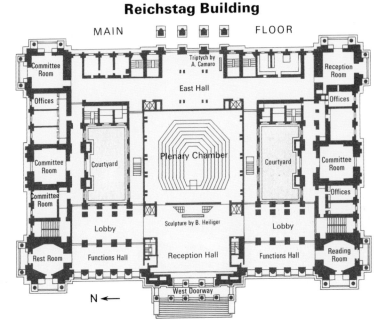

MAIN   FLOOR

building, "Questioning German History, from 1800 to the Present Day" (film shows, etc.).

The dome, blown up in 1957 as being in danger of collapse, has not been rebuilt; nor has the rich sculptural decoration been restored. The building has a Plenary Chamber seating 650, 30 committee rooms and almost 200 office rooms, which are used for meetings of committees of the Bundestag and Bundesrat (the two houses of the German Parliament) and of members of the various parties in Parliament. Visitors are catered for by a restaurant and a cafeteria.

Schöneberg Town Hall (Rathaus Schöneberg)   C4

Schöneberg Town Hall, still known by that name though it no longer serves as such, is the seat of the Chief Burgomaster of Berlin and of the House of Representatives, as well as the administrative centre of the city's 11th ward. The building was badly damaged during the last war; rebuilding was completed in 1952.

To the left of the main entrance is a tablet commemorating US President John F. Kennedy, and in the lobby is a portrait bust by Karl Trumpf of Friedrich Ebert, first President of the Weimar Republic. The square in front of the Town Hall, formerly called Rudolf-Wilde-Platz after the first Burgomaster of Schöneberg,

Location
John-F.-Kennedy-Platz, Schöneberg

U-Bahn
Rathaus Schöneberg

Buses
4, 16, 73, 74, 85

Schöneberg Town Hall

was renamed John-F.-Kennedy-Platz after the President's assassination in 1963.

In the 70 m (230 ft) high tower of the Town Hall is the Liberty Bell, a gift from the United States. The bell, a copy of the Liberty Bell in Philadelphia, was presented to Berlin by General Lucius D. Clay on United Nations Day (24 October) 1950. The cost of the bell was met by 17 million Americans, whose signatures are contained in a book preserved in the document room in the tower. The bell is 2·25 m (7½ ft) high and weighs 10 tons.

The bell is rung at noon every day and on special occasions. To the Berliners it is a symbol of freedom, and porcelain replicas from the National Porcelain Manufactory (see that entry) are still presented to guests of the Berlin Senate.

Sculpture Gallery

See Dahlem Museums

Soviet Memorial (Sowjetisches Ehrenmal)   B4

Location
Strasse des 17. Juni,
Tiergarten

Buses
69, 83

Only tourist buses are allowed into the section of the Strasse des 17. Juni in which the Soviet Memorial stands: normal traffic is not admitted.

This memorial to the Soviet Army, constructed of marble from the old Reichskanzlei (Chancellery of the Reich: Hitler's headquarters), was erected on the territory of West Berlin, near the Brandenburg Gate, in 1945–46. It bears the bronze figure of a soldier of the Red Army with fixed bayonet. The statue is flanked by two Soviet tanks, said to be the first to reach Berlin in 1945.

Two soldiers of the Soviet Army mount guard at the memorial. The guard is changed daily, the new guard coming from East Berlin by way of the Sandkrugbrücke (bridge) in Invaliden- strasse.

---

*Spandau Citadel (Zitadelle Spandau)

B2

Spandau Citadel is an imposing example of 16th c. Italian military engineering. (The Italians were the first to adopt the high-walled acute-angled bastion in place of the round bastion which had previously been employed.) Since 1977 restoration work has been in progress.

Location
Am Juliusturm, Spandau

U-Bahn
Zitadelle

Buses
13, 54

Opening times
Tue.–Fri. 9 a.m.–4.30 p.m.;
Sat., Sun. 10 a.m.–4.30 p.m.
Guided tours of historic
parts: Sat. 2–4 p.m., Sun.
10 a.m.–4 p.m.

The site was originally occupied by a moated castle belonging to the Askanier (the early ruling house of Brandenburg) and later by a frontier fortress erected by Albert the Bear (12th c.). The present citadel was begun by the Elector Joachim II in 1560 to protect his capital of Berlin. The architects were Christoph Römer and a Venetian, F. Chiaramella di Gandino, and from 1578 Count Rochus zu Lynar, who completed the stronghold in 1594. Since then, apart from a few modern alterations, it has remained unchanged. Entirely surrounded by water, the citadel is square in plan with a bastion at each corner (the King, Queen, Brandenburg and Crown Prince Bastions). At the time of its construction the citadel was impregnable. Thereafter it played a part in all the wars in which Brandenburg and Prussia were involved, and in the 17th and 18th c. was an important element in the Brandenburg defence system. During the Thirty Years War it was occupied by Swedish troops without a blow being struck, after negotiations between Gustavus Adolphus of Sweden and the Brandenburg Minister, Count Adam Schwarzenberg. During the Seven Years War, when Austrian forces invaded Brandenburg in 1757, the citadel provided a place of refuge for the Queen and the Court. In 1806 it was occupied by French forces, again without resistance, but was later recovered at the cost of bitter fighting.

A narrow bridge leads to the former command post (gatehouse; 16th c.) which received a new façade in 1849. In the pediment are carved and painted heraldic emblems of the provinces of Prussia at the beginning of the 18th c., surrounded by the ribbon of the English Order of the Garter. The Spandau Civic Museum of Local History is now housed on the first floor of the Command Building. In the basement is the Historic Inn.

Tour of the Citadel
Command Building

The gatehouse gives access to a spacious courtyard planted with chestnut trees and surrounded by buildings of many different periods (now housing the College of Building Crafts). On the right is a memorial to Margrave Albert the Bear.

Courtyard

Half left of the Command Building stands the Palas, built about 1350 and rebuilt at the beginning of the 16th c. In the lower part of the wall on the south side can be seen Jewish tombstones (13th–14th c.) with inscriptions in Hebrew. They came from

Palas

Spandau Citadel

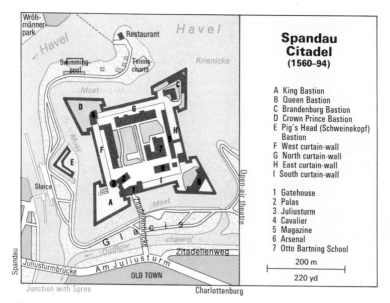

Spandau Citadel
(1560–94)

A King Bastion
B Queen Bastion
C Brandenburg Bastion
D Crown Prince Bastion
E Pig's Head (Schweinekopf) Bastion
F West curtain-wall
G North curtain-wall
H East curtain-wall
I South curtain-wall

1 Gatehouse
2 Palas
3 Juliusturm
4 Cavalier
5 Magazine
6 Arsenal
7 Otto Bartning School

200 m
220 yd

the Spandau Jewish cemetery which was laid bare about 1510, and the tombstones were used as building material when the Palas was refashioned. In the Palas are archives from the Municipal Museum of Local History. The hall has a wooden beamed ceiling.

The Juliusturm, to the rear of the Palas, is the oldest surviving part of the Citadel; it was built as the castle keep at the beginning of the 14th c. In 1874 Bismarck used it for the safe-keeping of Germany's war reserve, amounting to 120 million gold marks, and it continued to serve this purpose until 1919. The name of the tower is probably a corruption of Judenturm (Jew's Tower), for in 1356 Margrave Ludwig granted the lucrative office of Keeper of the Tower to a Court servant named as "the Jew Fritz". From the top of the tower (145 steps) there are magnificent views.

Juliusturm (Julius Tower)

The casemates in the King Bastion have been restored and are open to the public. The Great Powder Magazine (Grosses Pulvermagazin) contains various fragments and monuments of old Berlin, including the busts which formerly stood in the Victory Avenue in the Tiergarten (see entry).

Casemates

At the NW corner of the citadel is the King Bastion (Bastion König), with the Cavalier, a massive semicircular platform for heavy artillery. To the N is the Brandenburg Bastion, on which are the ruins of a gas protection laboratory of the Second World War. The small courtyard of the bastion is attractive, with its picturesque supporting arch (1814–43).
There are periodic exhibitions on the history of the citadel in the Palas. From the citadel there are pleasant walks alongside the moat (Zitadellengraben), with views of the River Havel.

Bastions

---

*Tegel Airport (Flughafen Berlin-Tegel)   B3/4

Tegel Airport has had a varied history. At first it was an army shooting-range, then a training ground for airship crews, and finally (from 1930) a rocket testing area. During the Berlin Blockade of 1948 it was used by the aircraft bringing in supplies in the famous Berlin air-lift, and for this purpose it was extended by the construction of runways. Some time later it became a French military airfield, which from 1960 was also used for civil flights (Air France).
The development of the airport to its present size began in 1969. In October 1974 the new Tegel Airport was inaugurated, and on 1 September 1975 it came into full operation.
Tegel has two runways, respectively 2400 m (2625 yds) and 3000 m (3280 yds) long, a hexagonal airport building and 15 gates, with a capacity of 15 million passengers. The apron can accommodate up to 30 aircraft.
Viewing terrace. Exhibition of old aircraft.

Location
Reinickendorf

Buses
8, 9 (city Bus) from Osloer Strasse or Zoo Station
Airport service

---

*Tegel House (Schloss Tegel)   A3

About 1550 the Elector Joachim II had a country residence at Tegel, later used by the Great Elector as a hunting-lodge. In

Location
Adelheid-Allee 19–21, Tegel

Tegel House

The new Tegel Airport

Tegel House

1765 it passed into the hands of the Humboldt family (whose descendants still own it), and in 1822–24 it was rebuilt in Neo-Classical style for Wilhelm von Humboldt by Karl Friedrich Schinkel. The four corner towers were designed by C. D. Rauch. The house is now a museum, with a rich collection of sculpture, pictures and graphic art.

From the house an avenue of lime trees leads to the mausoleum of the Humboldt family, built by Schinkel for Wilhelm von Humboldt after the death of his wife Karoline in 1829. In the centre is a granite Ionic column with a copy of Thorvaldsen's "Hope".

The park was originally laid out in 1792 as a Baroque garden, but was remodeled by Schinkel 32 years later as a landscaped park. It covers an area of 17·5 hectares (43 acres), and contains some fine old trees. In the northern part is an expanse of typical Brandenburg mixed forest (Nature Reserve).

The house and park can be easily reached by water, taking a boat of the Stern- und Kreisschiffahrt line to the Greenwich-Promenade landing-stage and continuing on foot through beautiful trees and past the Humboldt Hospital (turn right) to the house. This walk takes the visitor through the whole length of the park.

Alternatively, start from Tegel Underground station and walk through Alt-Tegel (to the left) to the riverside road (landing-stage); then turn right over the Tegeler Fliess (river) and continue to the hospital; then as above. Opposite the landing-stage is the island of Hasselwerder.

U-Bahn
Tegel

Buses
13, 14, 15, 20

Boat landing-stage
Greenwich-Promenade

Opening times
House and Park: May–Aug.
2–5.30 p.m.

Park

Telecommunications Tower (Fernmeldeturm)   D1

The 212 m (696 ft) high Telecommunications Tower stands in grounds of 10,000 sq. m (11,000 sq. yd) on the Schäferberg (103 m (338ft)), between the Wannsee and Glienicke Palace (see entries). It belongs to a directional radio station, and has large dish aerials, a steel lattice tower 45 m (148 ft) high and two parabolic aerials 10 m (33 ft) in diameter. The tower has three xenon lamps with a total strength of 40 million candlepower, which with the help of rotating lenses can be seen 200 km (125 miles) away. The installation carries Berlin's telecommunications traffic, linking up with other stations at Torfhaus in the Harz and Höhbeck on the Elbe. These stations also carry the second and third television channels. The tower is not open to the public.

Location
Zehlendorf
(Wannsee)

Bus
6

Tempelhof Airport (Flughafen Berlin-Tempelhof)   C5

In earlier times the area of the present airport was a military training ground. In 1883 the Swiss painter Arnold Böcklin experimented here with two motorless biplanes, but his attempts to fly failed because of high winds; then in 1908 the brothers Orville and Wilbur Wright achieved the first powered flight here (19 minutes).

In 1923 the airport began to operate for civil flights, and was extended in subsequent years, notably between 1936 and 1939 by the architect Ernst Sagebiel.

Location
Tempelhof

U-Bahn
Platz der Luftbrücke

Buses
4, 19, 24, 96

Air-Lift Memorial, Tempelhof Airport

Tempelhof was taken over by the American military government in 1945 as a military airport, and was not returned to civil use until 1950. In the following year the new Tempelhof Airport was brought into operation, and in 1962 the present terminal building (100 m (330 ft) by 50m (165 ft); 17 m (56 ft high)) was opened.

Since 1975 all Berlin's civil air traffic has been handled by Tegel Airport (see that entry), and Tempelhof is used only by the American authorities. All the installations at Tempelhof remain fully functional; but it gave place to Tegel as Berlin's main airport because of its situation within the city area, which made it impossible to contemplate any extension of the runways.

Air-Lift Memorial

In the Platz der Luftbrücke (Air-Lift Square) in front of the main entrance to Tempelhof Airport is the Air-Lift Memorial, commemorating the Berlin Blockade of 1948–49 and the Allied air-lift which brought in supplies to the beleagured city. The monument (by Eduard Ludwig, 1951) is 20 m (65 ft) high, with three towering arches symbolising the three air corridors which linked Berlin with West Germany during the Soviet blockade. The air-lift cost 77 lives (41 British, 31 Americans and 5 Berliners).

Teufelsberg C3

Location
Grunewald
(Wilmersdorf)

From either bus stop or from the S-Bahn station Grunewald it is a 20-minute walk to the recreation area at the N end of the Grunewald (see entry). The Teufelsberg (Devil's Hill) is a huge mound, 115 m (377 ft) high, built up from 25 million cu. m (33 million cu. yds) of rubble from the destroyed buildings of Berlin, on a site formerly occupied by the Faculty of Military Science. From the top of the hill, which is planted with trees of many different species (maple, alder, poplar, robinia, etc.), there are fine views. Recreation facilities include a toboggan-run, an Alpine crag for rock-climbers, a ski-jump and a launching area for model gliders.

S-Bahn
Grunewald

Buses
94 (Preussenallee)
69 (Schildhornweg)

---

*Tiergarten   B4 (a IV)

The Tiergarten (Animal Garden) – not to be confused with the Zoo (see entry) – was originally an Electoral hunting reserve in which deer, wild pigs and other game were preserved. About 1700 the Elector Frederick III began to transform the wooded country into a park, and caused a road to be built connecting it with Charlottenburg Palace. Frederick the Great had it laid out in the French style, while his successor Frederick William II converted it into an English-style landscaped park. In spite of these changes, however, much of the area of the Tiergarten remained in its natural unspoiled state.

At the end of the 19th c. the famous landscape-architect P. J. Lenné made the Tiergarten into a public park in the English manner.

Destroyed during the Second World War, its trees felled by Berliners seeking wood for fuel, the Tiergarten was replanted from 1949 onwards, the first tree – a young lime – being planted by Ernst Reuter, West Berlin's first Chief Burgomaster. It is now attractively laid out with an abundance of trees and shrubs, expanses of grass and flower borders.

The Tiergarten was formerly traversed from N to S by the Siegesallee (Victory Avenue), which was lined with numerous statues and monuments. Many of these suffered damage during the war; the remains are now preserved in Spandau Citadel (see entry). The most notable of the surviving figures are the following:

Monument to Goethe
This marble figure by F. Schaper was unveiled in 1880. On the base are allegorical female figures representing lyric poetry (with Amor), drama (a spirit bearing the symbol of death) and science.

Statue of Queen Luise
The statue, in white marble (by Erdmann Encke. 1880), depicts the Queen in a long high-waisted dress. On the circular base is a high relief recalling her work for the care of wounded soldiers during the War of 1806–07: it shows scenes from military life and women tending the wounded.

Monument to Frederick William III
The monument, by Friedrich Drake, was unveiled in 1849. The high reliefs on the upper part of the circular base depict the blessings of peace, reflecting the King's peace-loving disposition.

There are also statues of the 18th c. critic and philosopher Lessing (by O. Lessing, 1890), the composer Albert Lortzing

Location
Tiergarten

S-Bahn
Tiergarten, Bellevue

U-Bahn
Hansaplatz

Buses
16, 23, 24, 48, 69, 83

In the Tiergarten

(by G. Eberlein, 1906) and the novelist Theodor Fontane (by M. Klein, 1910).

To the S of the Congress Hall (see entry) is a work of modern sculpture in bronze, Henry Moore's "Two Forms".

20 July 1944 Memorial (Denkmal für die Opfer des 20. Juli 1944)   B4

Location
Stauffenbergstrasse 14,
Tiergarten

Buses
24, 29, 48, 75, 83

In the courtyard of the old War Office (Oberkommando der Wehrmacht) is a memorial to the officers (Generals Beck and Olbricht, Colonels von Stauffenberg and Mertz von Quirnheim, Lieutenant von Haeften) who were court-martialled and shot after the unsuccessful attempt on Hitler's life on 20 July 1944. The statue (by Richard Scheibe, 1953) depicts a young man in fetters.

On the second floor of the building is a memorial room devoted to the German resistance to Nazism within Germany and in other countries.

Urania   C4

Location
Kleiststrasse 13–14;
An der Urania (Schöneberg)

The Urania was established in 1888 by the industrialist Werner von Siemens and the astronomer Max Wilhelm Meyer as a place where the ordinary citizens of Berlin could find facilities

Victory Column ▶

U-Bahn
Wittenbergplatz

Buses
19, 29, 60, 69, 73, 85

for continuing their education, broadening their minds or pursuing special interests. The lectures, film shows, illustrated talks and discussions organised at the Urania cover a very wide range; anyone can join the association, but all events are open to non-members, who can obtain the programme on application.

The Urania was originally in Taubenstrasse, which is now in East Berlin. After the Second World War it was re-established in West Berlin and housed in a modern building, with lecture rooms, club-rooms and exhibition halls, near Tauentzienstrasse, a favourite Berlin shopping street.

Victory Column (Siegessäule) B4 (a IV)

Location
Grosser Stern, Tiergarten

Buses
16, 24, 69

Opening times
Tues–Sun 9 a.m.–6 p.m.
Mon. 1 p.m.–6 p.m.

The Victory Column stands in the centre of a large square between Ernst-Reuter-Platz and the Brandenburg Gate. Originally commissioned in 1865, it was ceremonially inaugurated on 2 September 1873, the anniversary of the German victory at Sedan, with a great military parade attended by the Emperor William I and his Generals. It commemorates the three victorious wars of 1864 against Denmark, 1866 against Austria and 1870–71 against France.

The shaft of the column incorporates a large number of canon-barrels captured from the enemy. The column stands on a high granite plinth with bronze reliefs depicting scenes from the three wars. On the base of the column, which is enclosed within an open colonnade, is a mosaic (by Anton von Werner) symbolising the achievement of German unity in 1870–71.

The column is crowned by a gilded figure of the goddess Victory holding the symbols of victory. The figure, more than 8 m (26 ft) high, was the work of Friedrich Drake.

The column, which has a total height of 67 m (220 ft), can be climbed by means of a spiral staircase. At a height of 48 m (157 ft) is an observation platform from which there are panoramic views. Until 1938 the Victory Column, together with statues of Bismarck, Moltke and Roon, stood in what is now the Platz der Republik.

Wannsee C/D1/2

Location
Zehlendorf

S-Bahn
Wannsee

Buses
3, 6, 18

Boat landing-stage
Wannsee Station (shuttle service)

Wannsee means two things to Berliners. On the one hand it is the residential district of Wannsee with its fine old villas set in large gardens – one of the best addresses in Berlin. On the other it is the lake of that name, or rather the two lakes, the Grosser and the Kleiner (Great and Little) Wannsee. The Wannsee ranks with the Grunewald (see entry) as one of the two great recreation areas of the Berliners – with the largest lido in Berlin and a range of other beaches, with sailing and rowing clubs, etc., with cafés and restaurants overlooking the Grosser Wannsee round its shores and with a variety of attractive footpaths and walks. Cut off as they are from the country surrounding the city, the people of Berlin flock in their thousands to "their" lake, the Wannsee.

The district of Wannsee is the largest of the old areas of settlement within Berlin. It consists of three parts which were amalgamated in 1899 – the colony round the station; the villa

Lido, Wannsee

colony of Alsen on the W side of the Wannsee, established in 1863; and the village of Stolpe on the Stölpchensee. Stolpe, which first appears in the records in 1299, has an old church, rebuilt in 1859 by Friedrich August Stüler, with a new carillon installed in 1958. In Bismarckstrasse, on the Kleiner Wannsee, is the tomb of the dramatist Heinrich von Kleist, who together with Henriette Vogel committed suicide here in 1811.

The Grosser Wannsee, which has an area of 260 hectares (640 acres), is part of a basin gouged out during the Ice Age. Its N end runs into the River Havel with its international shipping traffic. From its southern end (with the Wannsee Bridge, which carries the Königstrasse from Berlin to Potsdam) a string of small lakes connected with one another runs SW in a long trough also dating from the Ice Age – the Kleiner Wannsee, the Pohlesee, the Stölpchensee (bathing beach), the Prinz-Friedrich-Leopold-Kanal, the Griebnitzsee. The frontier with the German Democratic Republic follows the SW shore of the Griebnitzsee, and from its eastern end the Teltow Canal (Teltowkanal) runs E.

From Wannsee there are boats to Kladow (BVG line) and to Spandau Citadel (Stern- und Kreisschiffahrt). The landing-stages are below Wannsee Station (summer and winter timetables).

**Zoo (Zoologischer Garten)   B4 (a IV)

The Zoo lies right in the centre of Berlin, by the Zoo Station. Following their destruction during the last war the Zoo and the

Zoo

Location
Hardenbergplatz (main entrance),
Budapester Strasse (side entrance),
Tiergarten

U- and S-Bahn
Zoologischer Garten

Buses
9, 19, 29, 54, 60, 69, 73, 90, 94

Opening times
Daily 9 a.m. to dusk or 7 p.m., whichever is earlier

associated Aquarium have been reconstructed on the most modern principles so as to display the animals in their natural environment. The success achieved in breeding animals, including some rare species, demonstrates the success of the new methods. A visit to the Zoo and the Aquarium (at least half a day required) is accordingly an item to be included in every visitor's programme.

The history of the Zoo began in 1841, when King Frederick William IV presented to the city of Berlin his pheasantry in the Tiergarten and all the animals on the Pfaueninsel (see entry), together with their cages and animal houses, as the basis of a municipal zoo. The Zoo – the first in Germany – was opened in August 1844, with some 100 species, under the direction of a part-time board whose members included Alexander von Humboldt. A full-time professional Director was not appointed until 1869, in the person of Heinrich Bodinus. Finance was raised by the issue of shares, and a period of active development began. Bodinus died in 1884 and was succeeded as Director by Max Schmidt, who died after only four years' service and was in turn succeeded by Ludwig Heck. Under Heck's direction the development of the Zoo continued apace; the Elephant Gate in Budapester Strasse was among the buildings erected during this period.

The Aquarium, designed by Oskar Heinroth, was opened in 1913. Heck devoted much effort to increasing the number of species represented, making the Zoo one of the richest in the world. Retiring after 44 years as Director, he was succeeded by his son Lutz Heck, who sought to modernise the Zoo, introducing the first large open enclosures with no bars between the animals and spectators. By 1939 the Zoo had more than 4000 mammals and birds of some 1400 species.

After the war Katharina Heinroth became Director, and in 1956 she was succeeded by the present Director, Heinz-Georg Klös. Reconstruction continued, a notable development in 1975 being the house for nocturnal animals in the basement of the new Predator House. There are now about 9500 animals of 1800 species in the zoo.

The Aquarium was also enlarged and a fine new extension to the original building was opened at the end of 1980.

The best plan is to take a combined ticket for the Zoo and the Aquarium. Each adult visitor can take in, free of charge, a child under three. Children under ten are admitted only if accompanied by adults or older children. A permit, valid for the whole day, must be obtained for taking photographs.

In view of the size of the Zoo it is advisable to buy a guidebook at the ticket office.

The animal houses close at 6.30 p.m. from 1 May to 31 August, at 5.15 p.m. in March and from 1 to 15 October, at 6 p.m. in April and September and at 4.45 p.m. from 16 October to the end of February.

*Aquarium

The Aquarium has one of the largest collections of the kind in the world: its three storeys house some 6500 animals in 500 species. There are marine and fresh-water sections, a Crocodile Hall and an Insectarium, in which many of the animals are able to live in their natural environment.

East Berlin

Arms of
East Berlin

General

With an area of 403 sq. km (156 sq. miles) and a population of
more than 1·2 million, East Berlin is the largest city in the
German Democratic Republic and its political, economic and
intellectual centre.
The city is divided into eight wards, and borders the
administrative districts of Potsdam and Frankfurt an der Oder
(GDR) and West Berlin (Federal Republic).
East Berlin is the seat of government of the German Democratic
Republic, with the headquarters of the German Communist
Party and other State organisations. More than 120 foreign
embassies and trading agencies are based in the city.

Transport

Situated since time immemorial on important long-distance
trading routes, East Berlin is still an important centre of
international traffic. Its situation within the Berlin motorway
ring gives it good road connections in all directions.
Since the completion of the outer circle line in 1960 East Berlin
has been the principal railway junction in the German
Democratic Republic, with fast connections to all parts of the
country.
International air traffic is handled by Schönefeld Airport.
The city's waterways also play an important part in the
movement of goods and passengers.
Transport within the city is provided by a good S-Bahn
(suburban railway) system, two U-Bahn (Underground) lines,
trams and buses.

Culture

The old centre of Berlin lies in East Berlin, and now forms the
Mitte (Centre) ward of the city.
East Berlin is also the seat of renowned learned institutions
such as the Humboldt University, important technical colleges
and other higher educational establishments, and various
institutes and academies, and a noted centre of research and
teaching. Here, too, are the German National Library, more than
300 years old, the Central Pedagogical Library, one of the most
important specialised libraries in Europe, and world-famous
museums.
East Berlin is also reputed as a centre of theatrical art with a long
tradition.

Commerce and Industry

East Berlin is the largest industrial centre in the German
Democratic Republic, accounting for 6% of the country's total

Checkpoint Charlie

industrial output. Major elements in its industrial pattern are electrical engineering and electronics, engineering, clothing manufacture and foodstuffs.

Entry Points from West Berlin

There are entry points for day visits at Freidrichstrasse Station and Checkpoint Charlie (at Kochstrasse subway station). Motorists must carry their driving licence and car registration document. Visitors entering on foot or by U-Bahn must have a valid passport.
Make sure that your passport photograph is up to date. If you wear a beard or glasses and your photograph shows you without them you may be turned back at the frontier.

Visitors other than citizens of the Federal Republic of Germany

The entry points for pedestrians and motorists are at Bornholmer Strasse and Prinzenstrasse/Heinrich-Heine-Strasse, for those entering by S-Bahn or U-Bahn at Friedrich-strasse Station. West Germans may not use any other entry point.

Citizens of the Federal Republic of Germany

The entry points are open from 6 or 7 a.m. to midnight, but entry is permitted only until 8 p.m.

See also Practical Information, Entry into East Berlin.

◄ *Television Tower, East Berlin*

East Berlin from A to Z

Academy of Arts of the GDR (Akademie der Künste der DDR)   B4

Location
Hermann-Matern-
Strasse 58–59,
Berlin-Mitte

Bus
78

The Academy, successor in East Berlin to the Prussian Academy of Arts established in 1696, was refounded in 1950 with the general aim of fostering artistic creativity. It is divided into four sections – fine art, dramatic art, language and literature, music – and has over 100 members. It is the custodian of more than 70 collections of literary and artistic archives. The Academy puts on special exhibitions from time to time.

Academy of Sciences of the GDR   B5
(Akademie der Wissenschaften der DDR)

Location
Otto-Nuschke-
Strasse 22–23,
Berlin-Mitte

U-Bahn
Hausvogteiplatz

The Academy was originally founded in 1700 by Elector Frederick III, on the initiative of the philosopher Gottfried Wilhelm Leibniz, as the Brandenburg Society of Sciences, and was able to resume its activity, after the post-war turmoil, in 1946. Renamed the Academy of Sciences of the GDR in 1972, it now runs some 30 institutes concerned with fundamental research and has a staff of 15,000.

Outstanding figures associated with the Academy over the centuries have included Leonhard Euler, Albert Einstein, Jakob and Wilhelm Grimm, Alexander and Wilhelm von Humboldt, Max Planck and Rudolf Virchow.

---

*Alexanderplatz   B5

Location
Berlin-Mitte

U-Bahn
Alexanderplatz

S-Bahn
Alexanderplatz

Buses
9, 57, 78

The Alexanderplatz, so named in honour of Tsar Alexander of Russia in 1805, is now the centre of East Berlin life.

A hospice and a chapel dedicated to St George were built here, outside one of the town gates, at the end of the 13th c., and the gate was thereafter known as the Georgentor (St George's Gate). About 1700 a cattle market was established in this area, to be joined in the second half of the 18th c. by a wool market. In 1701 the Elector of Brandenburg, newly crowned King of Prussia, entered the town through St George's Gate, which was then renamed the King's Gate (Königstor) in his honour. In 1777 Frederick the Great built an imposing bridge here, with colonnades (built 1777–80) designed by Karl von Gontard.

The development of the square can be followed in eight porcelain panels in the pedestrian tunnel at the Hotel Stadt Berlin. They show (from left to right) the King's Gate in 1730, the cattle market on the counterscarp outside the King's Gate in 1780, the King's Bridge in 1785, the wool market in the Alexanderplatz in 1830, the Alexanderplatz about 1900, the square in 1930, the square in May 1945, as destroyed during the war, and the rebuilt square in autumn 1968.

There are many public buildings around the Alexanderplatz, reflecting its importance as a focal point of the city's life.

94

Alexanderplatz

On the site of a pre-war monument to Berlin, the Berolina Monument, there now stands a World Clock (Weltzeituhr).
The Centrum department store (by Josef Kaiser and Günter Kuhnert, 1967–70) is the largest in the German Democratic Republic – 78·60 m (258 ft) by 80·70 m (265ft); 34 m (112 ft) high.
The S-Bahn and U-Bahn stations, which suffered heavy destruction in 1945, were modernised after the war.
On the N side of the square is the Hotel Stadt Berlin, with 1000 rooms accommodating 2000 guests.
Other large buildings in the Alexanderplatz are the Ministry of Electrical Engineering and Electronics; the Teachers' House (Haus des Lehrers), the first new building erected in the square after 1945; and the GDR Travel Agency (Reisebüro der DDR).

The Alexanderplatz is a model of modern urban layout and traffic planning. Motor traffic is carried in tunnel and the trams are also kept out of the square, which is now a pedestrian precinct, while there are cafés to provide rest and refreshment for those whose business or pleasure takes them to the Alexanderplatz.

Archenhold Observatory (Archenhold-Sternwarte)   C6

The Archenhold Observatory in Treptow Park was founded by the astronomer Friedrich Simon Archenhold and was built in 1896 on the occasion of the Berlin Industrial Exhibition held in

Location
Alt-Treptow 1, Treptow

Arsenal

S-Bahn
Treptower Park

Buses
47, 64, 65, 66, 67

Opening times
Daily 2–5 p.m.

the park. In 1909 it was extended and completed to the design of Konrad Reimer and Friedrich Körte.

The Observatory's main attraction is its gigantic telescope, 21 m (69 ft) long. Since 1970 it has also housed a research unit concerned with the history of astronomy and the Zeiss Planetarium (frequent special lectures). There are conducted tours of the observatory (with an opportunity to look through the great telescope) and the Planetarium on Wednesdays at 6 and 8 p.m., Saturdays at 4 and 6 p.m. and Sundays at 4 p.m.

Arsenal (Zeughaus)   B5
(with Museum of German History)

Location
Unter den Linden 2,
Berlin-Mitte

U-Bahn
Hausvogteiplatz

S-Bahn
Friedrichstrasse,
Marx-Engels-Platz

Bus
57

Opening times
Mon.–Thu. 9 a.m.–6 p.m.,
Sat. and Sun. 10 a.m.–5 p.m.

Closed
Fri.

This fine Baroque building in Unter den Linden (15 minutes' walk from the U-Bahn and S-Bahn) now houses the Museum of German History.

The Arsenal was begun in 1695 to the design of Johann Arnold Nering and completed in 1706 by Martin Grünberg, Andreas Schlüter and Jean de Bodt. From 1730 to 1877 it was used for the storage of captured war material, and from 1880 (after internal reconstruction by Hitzig) as a Military Museum and a Hall of Fame celebrating the feats of the Brandenburg and Prussian armies.

The Arsenal building, on a square plan, has a clearly articulated façade (by de Bodt), 90 m (295 ft) long, which is relieved architecturally by projections and recesses. The cornices, balustrades and sculpture are in sandstone, the main structure in brick revetted with plaster. The ground floor has round-arched windows, while the narrow windows of the upper floor have alternately rounded and triangular pediments; some are topped by allegorical figures.

The Sculptural decoration of the exterior is by Schlüter, the 22 heads of dying warriors in particular being outstanding examples of German monumental sculpture. The four figures at the entrance are by the French scultor Guillaume Hulot. The four female figures on projecting bases at the main entrance represent Pyrotechnics, Arithmetic, Geometry and Mechanics. The building was badly damaged during the last war and was restored between 1948 and 1961 under the direction of Otto Haesler. The reopening was in 1965. Serenade concerts are given during the summer (end of June to August) in the Schlüter Courtyard (seats should be booked well in advance) under the auspices of the Konzert- and Gastspieldirektion der DDR, Johannisstrasse 2, 1040 Berlin.

Adjoining the main doorway is the entrance to a special commemorative exhibition, "Lenin in Berlin".

Museum of German History

This is the leading historical museum in the German Democratic Republic, concentrating particularly on the popular revolutionary movements of the 19th and 20th c. The material on display includes contemporary documents, books, pictures, maps, etc.

The Museum also illustrates the course of German history from early times to the establishment of the GDR after the Second World War. There are periodic special exhibitions on topical themes.

The Arsenal (Museum of German History)

detail

Marx-Engels Bridge between the Arsenal and the Cathedral

Berlin Palace (Berlin-Palais) B5

Location
Unter den Linden,
Berlin-Mitte

The Berlin Palace originated as the Crown Prince's Palace (Kronprinzenpalais), created by Johann Arnold Nering in 1663–64 by the conversion and alteration of a handsome existing town house. In 1732 this passed into the hands of King Frederick William I, who had it remodeled in Baroque style by Philipp Gerlach as a residence for the Crown Prince. It was later occupied by Prince Augustus William, Frederick the Great's brother, and from 1793 by Crown Prince Frederick William and his wife Luise.

In 1811 the Crown Prince's Palace was linked with the Princesses' Palace by a bridge designed by Heinrich Gentz. After further rebuilding and the construction of an additional storey by Johann Heinrich Strack the palace became the residence of the future Emperor Frederick III and his wife Victoria (daughter of Queen Victoria) in 1856, and here William II, the last German Emperor, was born on January 27 1859.

The palace was destroyed during the Second World War. No plans of the building had been preserved, and it was, therefore, rebuilt by Richard Paulick (1968–69) on the basis of the old prints. The Berlin Palace is now a House of Culture (arts centre) and guest-house. At the rear is the Schinkelklause Restaurant.

**Bode Museum B5

Location
Kupfergraben – Monbijou-
Brücke, Berlin-Mitte

S-Bahn
Friedrichstrasse, Marx-
Engels-Platz

Opening times
Wed.–Sun. 9 a.m.–6 p.m.
Fri. 10 a.m.–6 p.m.

The Bode Museum is situated at the northern end of the Museum Island, the old museum centre of Berlin. Frederick William IV had designated the island in the River Spree as "an open space for art and science".

The Museum is a development of the Kaiser Friedrich Museum which was opened in 1904. In 1956 it was renamed in honour of its founder, Wilhelm von Bode, who from 1872 until 1929 was its controller and who won great esteem from 1906 to 1920 as General Director of the Berlin Museums, when he was responsible for their development and extension.

The Neo-Baroque museum building dates from 1897–1904, the architect being Ernst von Ihne. In the domed Great Staircase there stands on its original plinth a bronze copy of Schluter's equestrian statue of the Great Elector (see Charlottenburg Palace); below the Little Dome in the rear staircase can be seen two groups by the sculptor Adriaen de Vries.

The Bode Museum comprises the Egyptian Museum, the Papyrus Collection, the Early Christian and Byzantine Collection, the Sculpture Collection, the Picture Gallery, the Museum of Prehistory and the Cabinet of Coins and Medals.

Egyptian Museum

The Egyptian Museum covers Egyptian history from prehistoric times to the Graeco-Roman period and contains many exhibits of outstanding quality.

The room devoted to death and burial illustrates the Egyptian cult of the dead. Items of particular interest include X-ray photographs of the mummies of a woman, an ibis (the bird sacred to the goddess Isis) and a jackal, numbers of other mummies and grave-goods. The bust of Queen Nefertiti formerly in this museum was removed for safe-keeping during

Bode Museum

the last war and is now in the Egyptian Museum in Charlottenburg, West Berlin (see entry).

The Papyrus Collection, with some 15,000 papyri, is one of the largest collections of the kind in the world.
In addition to Egyptian and Greek documents the collection also includes texts in Latin, Hebrew, Aramaic, Middle Persian, Syriac, Nubian and Amharic.

Papyrus Collection

This collection includes examples of the arts and crafts of the Mediterranean countries from the 3rd to the 18th c. The most notable exhibit is an apse mosaic in glass and marble from the Church of San Michele in Africisco, Ravenna (restored 1952). Other items of interest included portrait and monumental sculpture, icons, Coptic art, panel-paintings, funerary stelae, pottery and woollen and silk fabrics from Egyptian tombs.
Much applied art formerly in the collection was removed for storage in western Berlin during the war and is now in the Museum of Antiquities in West Berlin (see entry).

Early Christian and
Byzantine Collection

The Sculpture collection suffered heavy losses during the last war, and some of the collection is now in West Berlin (see Dahlem Museums, Sculpture Gallery).
The collection is particularly strong in architectural sculpture from Germany, the Low Countries, Venice and Florence.
Other fields well represented are German, Dutch and Flemish sculpture. There are some 450 works of sculpture of the Late Gothic period (figures supporting a pulpit, by Anton Pilgram; carved altar from Antwerp, etc.).
Particularly famous are the works by Italian masters and works

Sculpture Collection

Brandenburg Gate, with a view of the Television Tower in East Berlin

of the Late Gothic schools of South Germany and the Low Countries.

Picture Gallery

The Picture Gallery illustrates the development of painting in Germany and the Low Countries from the 15th to the 18th c., and also includes examples of 18th c. English and French painting. In accordance with a principle established by Bode, period furniture and sculpture of the various periods are also displayed.

Museum of Prehistory

A selection of exhibits from this museum is displayed from time to time.

Cabinet of Coins and Medals

This is one of the largest collections of the kind in the world, containing half a million items dating from every period and illustrating the development of coining techniques from antiquity to the present day. Only a small proportion of the total holdings of coins, medals, banknotes and seals can be put on display at any one time.

**Brandenburg Gate (Brandenburger Tor)   B4

Bus
9

S-Bahn
Friedrichstrasse

The Brandenburg Gate, symbol of the divided city, has been inaccessible from West Berlin since the construction of the Berlin Wall in 1961, since it now lies beyond the boundary between the two halves of Berlin.

The Gate, modelled on the Propylaea on the Acropolis of

Athens, was built for King Frederick William II in 1788–91 by Carl Gotthard Langhans the Elder as a suitably magnificent terminal feature at the West end of Unter den Linden (see entry). The first Neo-Classical structure in Berlin, it was opened to traffic on 6 August 1791 in presence of the King. It is 20 m (65 ft) high, 62 m (203 ft) wide and 11 m (36 ft) deep.

There are six Doric columns on each side, forming five passages. The wider central passage was reserved for the carriages of the Court; the other four were used by ordinary traffic.

On top of the Gate is the Quadriga by Johann Gottfried Schadow, a four-horse chariot driven by the goddess of Victory, who holds the symbols of victory. Originally the goddess was naked, but this gave rise to so much moral indignation on the one hand, and so many ribald jokes on the other, that Schadow felt compelled to clothe her in a decent garment of sheet-copper.

After Napoleon's defeat of Prussia he carried the Quadriga off to Paris. After the Wars of Liberation it was returned to its original place, to the great delight of the Berliners.

In the Second World War the Brandenburg Gate was severely damaged; after restoration in West Berlin the Quadriga was replaced in 1958.

*Cathedral (Dom)   B5

Berlin Cathedral, designed by Julius Raschdorff in the style of the Italian High Renaissance, was built in 1894–1905 on the site of an earlier cathedral dating from the time of Frederick the Great (1750). Standing 85 m (280 ft) high, it suffered severe destruction during the Second World War but in recent years has been undergoing careful restoration.

The Hohenzollern Vault (Hohenzollerngruft: not open to the public) contains the tombs of the Great Elector and his wife Dorothea, Frederick I and his wife Sophie Charlotte, Frederick William II and other members of the family

The cathedral is open to visitors from Monday to Wednesday and Friday noon to 4 p.m., and Saturday 10 a.m.–1 p.m.

Location
Marx-Engels-Platz

S-Bahn
Marx-Engels-Platz

Charité Hospital   B4

The Charité Hospital, founded by King Frederick I in 1710, occupies an area of 147,000 sq. m (275 acres) bounded by Invalidenstrasse, Robert-Koch-Platz, Hermann-Matern-Strasse and Schumannstrasse. It has 2000 beds and handles some 250,000 cases a year, including more than 30,000 in-patient cases. It was originally established as a plague hospital, but since Berlin and the surrounding area escaped the plague it was converted into a general hospital, undergoing reconstruction for this purpose between 1785 and 1797. When Berlin University was founded in 1810 senior doctors and teachers of the Charité clinics and institutes became professors. In its first year the medical faculty had 117 students, and its first Dean was Christoph Wilhelm Hufeland, who introduced smallpox vaccination.

Location
Schumannstrasse 20–21, Berlin-Mitte

S-Bahn
Friedrichstrasse

Bus
78

Among those who practised and taught at the Charité were Rudolf Virchow, Robert Koch, Ferdinand Sauerbruch and Theodor Brugsch, who became Director of the hospital after 1945. Between 1933 and 1945 the Nazis expelled, persecuted or murdered 138 members of the faculty of medicine.

During the last war the Charité suffered severe destruction, and reconstruction, which will make it one of the most modern hospitals in the world, is still in progress. In March 1981 the first part of the new surgical centre, a diagnostic department, was completed, and this now has a capacity of 215,000 investigations a year. This surgical centre (24 operating theatres) is the largest project so far undertaken by the GDR Health Service.

Crown Prince's Palace

See Berlin Palace

East Asian Collection

See Pergamon Museum

Egyptian Museum

See Bode Museum

The Humboldt University, with a monument to its founder, Wilhelm von Humboldt

Folk Museum

See Pergamon Museum

Humboldt University (Humboldt-Universität)   B5

The building occupied by the Humboldt University was originally erected by J. Boumann in 1748–66, to the design of Georg Wenzeslaus von Knobelsdorff, as a palace for Frederick the Great's brother Prince Henry; but in 1810 Frederick William III made it over to the University which had been founded by Wilhelm von Humboldt. Humboldt wrote in 1809: "The University in Berlin, which is now really decided on, with the two Academies and all the institutes, the library, the observatory, the art gallery, etc., are to be brought together in one large institution. The King is giving them a substantial sum by way of revenue, settled on real estate but to be paid in full only gradually, as the finances improve, and he is presenting to the University Prince Henry's palace and to the Academy the whole building, of which up to now it possessed only half."
The University was accordingly named the Frederick William University after its royal benefactor. The King was concerned to demonstrate, during the period of French occupation, that "although we have lost some of our physical power, we still possess our intellectual power."
In 1949 the University was renamed the Humboldt University after its founder.
In the gardens in front of the University are monuments to distinguished scholars. Among those who have taught at the university are Hegel, Schleiermacher, the brothers Grimm, Helmholtz, Mommsen, Planck, Einstein, and the doctors Virchow, Koch and Sauerbruch.

Location
Unter den Linden,
Berlin-Mitte

S-Bahn
Friedrichstrasse

Bus
57

Islamic Museum

See Pergamon Museum

*Köpenick Palace (Schloss Köpenick) and   C7
Museum of Applied Art (Kunstgewerbemuseum)

Köpenick Palace occupies the site of a medieval Slav stronghold which is thought to have been the residence of Prince Jacza de Copnic. In the mid 16th c. the old moated castle, then ruinous, gave place to a Renaissance-style hunting-lodge built by the Elector Joachim II. During the Thirty Years War King Gustavus Adolphus of Sweden took up his quarters here. Then at the end of the 17th c. the Great Elector had the house rebuilt in its present form by Rutger van Langevelt. In 1730 the palace was the venue of the court-martial, ordered by Frederick William I, of Crown Prince Frederick (later Frederick the Great) and his friend Lieutenant von Katte, who had helped Frederick in his attempt to escape

Location
Schlossinsel, Köpenick

S-Bahn
Spindlersfield

Buses
16, 25, 26, 62, 84

Opening times
Wed.–Sat. 9 a.m.–5 p.m.;
Sun. 10 a.m.–6 p.m.

Köpenick Palace

from his father's control. Von Katte was condemned to death and, on the King's orders, executed in front of the Crown Prince.

From 1849 to 1926 the palace was occupied by a teachers' training college.

In an annex to the main building is a small gallery used for special exhibitions of work by contemporary artists. Concerts are held in the palace chapel which was designed by Johann Arnold Nering.

The park, which contains rare species of trees, was laid out in the 19th c. and has recently been reconstructed by Helmut Lichy.

Museum of Applied Art

The Museum of Applied Art, originally founded in 1867, has been housed in the palace since 1963. Its Baroque interior, with magnificent stucco ceilings, provides a handsome setting for the collection of furniture, pottery and porcelain, glass, goldsmith's work, metalwork, leather articles, etc., which gives an excellent survey of 900 years of European applied art, from the Middle Ages to the present day.

---

*Marienkirche (St Mary's Church)   B5

Location
Karl-Liebknecht-Strasse,
on the Neuer Markt,
Berlin-Mitte

The Marienkirche is Berlin's oldest surviving parish church and was only the second parish church to be established in the town. It is the church in which the Bishop of Berlin preaches. The church first appears in the records in 1294. It was burned down in 1380 but was rebuilt a few years later. The aisleless choir with the two-storey crypt chapel was built three centuries later (1659–63). The Neo-Gothic steeple by Christian Gotthard Langhans was added in 1789–90.

The plain exterior of the church gives no hint of the treasures within. A particularly notable feature is a fresco of the Dance of Death (2 m (6½ ft) high, 22·6 m (74 ft) long), probably painted after an outbreak of plague in 1484. It is much faded as a result of environmental pollution.

In front of the entrance is an expiatory cross recalling the murder of Provost Nikolaus von Bernau. The bronze font dates from 1437. The fine Baroque pulpit in the nave is by Andreas Schlüter. The organ recitals given in the church attract large audiences.

Opening times
Mon.–Fri. 8.30 a.m.–midday and 1–5 p.m., Sat. midday–5 p.m., Sun. midday–1 p.m.

S- and U-Bahn
Alexanderplatz

Bus
57

*Marx-Engels-Platz   B5

The Marx-Engels-Platz (Marx-Engels Square) has borne its present name only since 1951. Before then it was known as the Lustgarten (Pleasure Garden), recalling its origin as a botanic garden. Originally laid out in 1573 as a herb and kitchen garden, it was transformed in 1643 into an ornamental garden, in which the first potatoes in Prussia were grown in 1649. Thereafter it gradually changed its aspect. In the reign of Frederick William I it became a military parade-ground; the first trees were planted in the 1830s; and thereafter the first large buildings were erected.

The Lustgarten lay at the centre of old Berlin. After 1945 the square was enlarged by the demolition of the old Berlin Palace and was used for mass rallies and parades. It now looked very different from the pre-war Lustgarten. In 1964 the building now occupied by the National Council (Staatsrat) of the GDR was built on the S side of the square, incorporating in its N front the doorway of the old Palace, from the balcony of which Karl Liebknecht proclaimed a Socialist Republic in 1918. The W side of the square, beyond the Spree, is occupied by the massive Foreign Ministry. To the N, opposite the National Council building, is the Cathedral. The N end of the square is flanked by the Old Museum, to the W of which is the Arsenal.

Location
Berlin-Mitte

S-Bahn
Marx-Engels-Platz

Buses
9, 57, 78

Opposite the Foreign Ministry of the DDR, on the former site of the City Castle, stands the Palace of the Republic (1973–76). It is a prestigious glassed-in building, 180 m (590 ft) long, which houses the Volkskammer (People's Chamber) and which also serves as a community and cultural centre. On the ground floor of the entrance hall, which extends upwards through several storeys, are an information centre and a post office; in the upper part of the entrance hall is the "Galerie im Palast". The main hall has seating for 5000 and there are also a theatre, club-rooms and several places for rest and refreshment.

Palace of the Republic

The Marx-Engels Bridge, constructed 1822–24 by Schinkel as the "Castle Bridge", leads from the north-west corner of the square over an arm of the Spree to the street called Unter den Linden. On the pillars surmounting the piers can be seen sculpture groups, created between 1845 and 1847 to designs by Schinkel, which were returned to East Berlin by West Berlin in 1981.

Marx-Engels Bridge
(picture on p. 97)

Molkenmarkt and Ministry of Culture   B4

Location
Berlin-Mitte

U-Bahn
Klosterstrasse

Bus
9

The Molkenmarkt (Whey Market), known in the Middle Ages as the Old Market, was the site of the first settlement which grew to become Berlin. The first Town Hall was built here, and from this square the oldest river-crossing, the Mühlendamm (Mill Causeway), spanned the River Spree to link Berlin and Cölln.

Here, too, stood the old Municipal Prison, which gave place in 1935 to the new Mint. The Mint and the adjoining Schwerin Palace (built in 1704 by Jean de Bodt) now house the Ministry of Culture. Along the front of the building is a frieze by Gottfried Schadow from the Schwerin Palace, copied by Schadow from a frieze by Friedrich Gilly on the old Mint.

*Müggelsee   C8

Location
Köpenick

S-Bahn
Friedrichshagen

Bus
27 (to Müggelberge)

The Müggelsee, in the SE of the city, is Berlin's largest lake, with an area of 7·5 sq. km (3 sq. miles) and a maximum depth of 8 m (26 ft). The 120 m (130 yd) long Spree Tunnel, opened in 1926, runs under the W end of the lake, linking the district of Friedrichshagen with the southern Müggelberge, the hills which surround the lake, and which rise to a height of 115 m (377 ft). The well-marked footpaths round the lake have a total length of 160 km (100 miles).

A particularly attractive walk is the ridge walk along the Müggelberge to the Müggelturm (Müggel Tower), with an inn and a magnificent view. There is also an interesting nature trail in the wooded area S of the lake, starting from the restaurant on the shores of the Teufelssee near the Müggelturm and passing over a stretch of moorland into the Müggelberge; tablets set at intervals along the trail, which is 3 km (2 miles) long, give information about the local plant and animal life. For those who want to explore the area more thoroughly a map showing the footpaths is available. There are several cafés available to walkers for rest and refreshment, e.g. Rübezahl, Müggelseeperle, Müggelturm, etc.

Museum of Applied Art

See Köpenick Palace

Museum of German History

See Arsenal

Museum of Prehistory

See Bode Museum

National Gallery

In the National Gallery

National Gallery (Nationalgalerie) B5

Location
Bodestrasse, Berlin-Mitte

S-Bahn
Marx-Engels-Platz

Opening times
Wed.–Sun. 9 a.m.–6 p.m.
Fri. 10 a.m.–6 p.m.

The National Gallery, originally built as a hall for receptions and other ceremonial occasions in 1866–76 (architects F. A. Stüler and J. H. Strack), is in the form of a Corinthian temple set on a high base and approached by an imposing flight of steps. In front of the building is a bronze equestrian statue of Frederick William IV by Alexander Calandrelli (1886). The female figures in the gardens are by Georg Kolbe.

The Collection of Modern Art (Sammlung Neue Kunst) consists of pictures and sculpture from the end of the 18th c. to the present day, including works by Arnold Böcklin, Lovis Corinth, Goya, Franz Krüger, Max Liebermann, Adolph von Menzel, Max Slevogt and Hans Thoma.

Part of the original collection is now in the New National Gallery in West Berlin (see entry).

The collection of Revolutionary and anti-Fascist art is in Otto Nagel Haus, Märkisches Ufer 16–18 (see Practical Information – Musuems).

National Library (Deutsche Staatsbibliothek) B5

Location
Unter den Linden 8,
Berlin-Mitte

S-Bahn
Friedrichstrasse

Opening times
Mon.–Fri. 9 a.m.–9 p.m.,
Sat. 9 a.m.–5 p.m.

Closed
Sun.

Conducted tours
First Sun. in month at
10.30 a.m.

Bus
57

The National Library in Neo-Baroque style, was built between 1903 and 1914 by Ernst von Ihnen, and was known until 1945 as the Prussian State Library. It measures 79 m (260 ft) by 105 m (345 ft).

The first "Electoral Library at Cölln on the Spree" was housed from 1661 in the so-called "Pharmacy Wing" of the Berlin Palace. In 1780 this gave place to the Old Library. Until 1902 the site of the present library was occupied by the headquarters of the Academy of Sciences and Academy of Arts, in which the philosopher Johann Gottlieb Fichte delivered his famous "Addresses to the German Nation" in 1807–08.

In 1939 the National Library had some 3,820,000 volumes, which were dispersed during the Second World War to more than 30 different places in Germany. The stock has now grown to 5,100,000 volumes. There are 12 reading-rooms, 430 desks for readers and a collection of 130,000 volumes available for immediate reference.

* Neue Wache (New Guardhouse) B5

Location
Unter den Linden,
Berlin-Mitte

Mounting of guard
Daily 2.30 p.m.

Changing of guard
Every hour on the hour

Bus
57

The Neue Wache was built by K. F. Schinkel in 1816–18 on the site of an earlier guardhouse: a massive brick structure preceded by a Doric portico in the manner of a Greek temple. In 1931 the interior was altered (architect Heinrich Tessenow) to serve as a memorial to the dead of the First World War. Within the main hall, the walls of which were faced with limestone slabs, stood a tall block of black granite, lit by a roof-light, on which lay a wreath of oak-leaves flanked by two perpetually burning candelabra.

Since 1960 the Neue Wache (altered in 1969) has been a memorial to the victims of Fascism and militarism. In the centre of the Hall of Honour, within a crystal cube, is the eternal flame, and below this are urns containing the ashes of unknown resistance fighters and the Unknown Soldier. On the side wall,

Memorial to the victims of Fascism and militarism (formerly Neue Wache)

in golden letters, are the words, "To the Victims of Fascism and Militarism".

A guard of honour is mounted in front of the Neue Wache by soldiers of the National People's Army. There is a short mounting of the guard ceremony at 2.30 p.m. every day, and the guard is changed every hour on the hour. There is a full ceremonial mounting of the guard at 2.30 p.m. on Wednesdays and public holidays, on Army Day and the memorial day for the victims of Fascism and militarism.

Nicolaihaus (Nicolai-Körner-Haus) B5

This house, now occupied by the National Monuments Board (Amt für Denkmalpflege), was built in the early 18th c., and some years later became the residence of the writer, critic and publisher Christoph Friedrich Nicolai, who also had his bookshop here.

The house, after alteration by the master-builder and musician C. F. Zelter, a friend of Nicolai (and also of Goethe), who is commemorated by a plaque, became the meeting-place of the intellectual élite of the day. Among those who frequented the house were the philosopher Moses Mendelssohn, the sculptor Gottfried Schadow, the writer Anna Luise Karsch and the celebrated draughtsman and etcher Daniel Chodowiecki.

After Nicolai's death in 1811 the bookshop passed into the hands of his son-in-law, the Court Counsellor Gustav Parthey. From Easter to May 1811 the dramatist Theodor Körner lived in

Location
Brüderstrasse 13,
Berlin-Mitte

U-Bahn
Spittelmarkt

Buses
9, 32, 78

the house. In 1814 it became the home of the writer Elise von der Recke, born Countess Meden, a sister of the reigning Duchess of Courland.
In 1892 the bookshop moved to Dorotheenstrasse.

Other houses in Brüderstrasse

No. 33 was once occupied by the architect Andreas Schlüter. At Brüderstrasse 10 is the Galgenhaus (Gallows House), built about 1680, where according to legend a maid was hanged for a theft she did not commit.

Nikolaikirche (St Nicholas's Church)   B5

Location
Nikolaikirchplatz,
Berlin-Mitte

The Nikolaikirche can be reached on foot by way of Rathausstrasse and Poststrasse.
This church, the oldest building in Berlin, was founded about 1200, and a hall church in Late Gothic style was built about 1470. Archaeological investigations in 1956–57 brought to light foundations and the remains of the churchyard. The great Protestant hymn-writer Paul Gerhardt was clergyman here from 1657 to 1666. The church was renovated by Karl Friedrich Schinkel in 1817. During the Second World War it suffered severe damage, and the rich furnishings were destroyed. The great 18th c. dramatist Gotthold Ephraim Lessing lived in the square in front of the church from 1752 to 1755. His tragedy "Miss Sara Sampson" was written at No. 10 (replaced in 1870 by a new building).
A thorough renovation of the old quarter around the Nikolaikirche is planned to begin in 1987.

Old Museum

*Old Museum (Altes Museum)   B5

The Old Museum, situated on the Museumsinsel (Museum Island), is Berlin's oldest museum and the oldest in Germany after the Glyptothek in Munich. Built by Karl Friedrich Schinkel in 1824–30, it is in the style of a Greek temple, with a portico of 18 Ionic columns. It was burned down during the Second World War, rebuilt in 1960 and reopened six years later.

The Old Museum contains the 20th century section of the National Gallery, also the collection and the study rooms of the Print Cabinet and the collection of drawings which are open to the public Monday to Friday 9 a.m.–midday and 1–5 p.m.

In the entrance hall are six figures by K. F. Schinkel from the Schlossbrücke (Palace Bridge) – "Nike crowning the victor", "Young man conducted into battle by Athena", "Nike conveying the dead victor to Olympus", etc. The figures were removed from the bridge during the Second World War for safe-keeping; after the war they were in West Berlin, but were returned to East Berlin in April 1981. They are temporarily housed in the museum pending their return to their original positions on the bridge.

On the ground floor of the museum (entrance from the street running past the Cathedral) is a large study room belonging to the Print Cabinet, which has a collection of 130,000 sheets of graphic art – miniatures, drawings, engravings, woodcuts, etchings, etc. – ranging in date from the 15th c. to the present day. It is thus one of the largest collections of the kind in Europe. On the first floor is a room for exhibitions.

Location
Marx-Engels-Platz,
Berlin-Mitte

Opening times
Wed.–Sun. 9 a.m.–6 p.m.
Fri. 10 a.m.–6 p.m.

Print Cabinet

Opera House

Opera House

During the last war the collection was dispersed, and much of it is now in West Berlin (see Dahlem Museums, Print Cabinet).

20th c. art

The gallery, opened in 1964, has since 1973 formed part of the new Centre for Art Exhibitions. This section covers the art of the period from 1900 to the present day, and contains works by members of Die Brücke group (see Brücke Museum in West Berlin) and the Neue Sachlichkeit (New Objectivity) movement and a large representation of works of social criticism and the period of resistance to Fascism.

Drawings

The collection contains some 40,000 drawings, water-colours and oil-studies, including almost all the drawings of the painter and draughtsman Adolph von Menzel and drawings by K. F. Schinkel and Karl Blechen.

Opera House (Deutsche Staatsoper)   B5

Location
Unter den Linden, Berlin-Mitte

S-Bahn
Friedrichstrasse

Bus
57

The Opera House was originally built by Georg Wenzeslaus von Knobelsdorff in the North German Neo-Classical style. It was the first theatre to be built in Germany which was not part of a palace.
In 1843 the Opera House was completely burned down, but was rebuilt a year later under the direction of C. F. Langhans. During the 1920s it was modernised. It was again completely destroyed during the Second World War, but rebuilding began in 1951 (architects Richard Paulick and Kurt Hemmerling), and

Operncafé

in September 1955 the new Opera House was inaugurated with a performance of Wagner's "Mastersingers".
The house has seating for 1480. The programme includes opera, ballet and concerts.

Operncafé   B5

The Operncafé is a faithful reproduction of the old Princesses' Palace, a two-storey Baroque building erected in 1733–37 (architect F. W. Dietrich) which was linked by an arched gateway with the Berlin Palace (see entry). The Princesses' Palace is so called because it was the residence until their marriage of the three daughters of Frederick William III.
The palace was destroyed during the last war and was rebuilt in 1961–63 (architect Richard Paulick) to accommodate the Operncafé (café concert, grill, wine restaurant, late-night bar; outdoor café in summer).
In front of the Operncafé, extending to the Opera House, is a public garden, with statues of Blücher, Gneisenau, Scharnhorst and Yorck – fine examples of Neo-Classical sculpture from the workshop of Christian Daniel Rauch.

Location
Unter den Linden,
Berlin-Mitte

S-Bahn
Karl-Marx-Platz

U-Bahn
Hausvogteiplatz

Bus
57

Parish Church (Parochialkirche)   B5

This centrally planned Baroque church, designed by J. A. Nering and built by the Court Architect, Ph. Grünberg, in

Location
Klosterstrasse, Berlin-Mitte

Pergamon Altar

Pergamon Museum

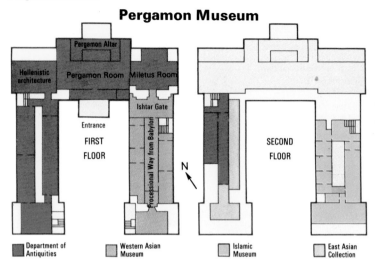

1695–1703, was severely damaged during the Second World War. The tower, designed by Jean de Bodt and built by Philipp Gerlach, survived the bombing; it contained a Dutch peal of 37 bells which rang for the first time in 1715 and for the last time in 1944. The church now contains an interesting collection of religious art.

Behind the church, in Waisenstrasse, is a fragment of Berlin's old town walls, dating from the 13th–14th c.

Pergamon Museum   B5

Location
Bodestrasse 1–3,
Berlin-Mitte

S-Bahn
Marx-Engels-Platz,
Friedrichstrasse (15-min.
walk)

The Pergamon Museum is entered by way of the bridge over the Kupfergraben.

One of the oldest museums of architecture in the world, it was designed by A. Messel and Ludwig Hoffman and built between 1903 and 1930, with a long interruption during the First World War.

The complex includes the Folk Museum, the Department of Antiquities, with the Pergamon Altar, the Western Asian Museum, the Islamic Museum and the East Asian Collection.

At least half a day should be allowed for a visit to the whole of the Pergamon Museum which is open daily 9 a.m. (Fri. 10 a.m.)–6 p.m.; Mon. and Tue. only Western Asian Museum and Architecture rooms of Department of Antiquities.

Folk Museum

The Museum für Volkskunde (Folk Museum), on the ground floor, displays furniture, household and other equipment, textiles, pottery and ceramic (Winterthur tiled stove, 1665), toys and other examples of folk arts and crafts also the "City Proletariat" collection.

In the museum is a memorial to the teacher Adolf Reichwein, executed on 20 October 1944.

The Museum has a branch at Breitscheidstrasse 8, Wandlitz, with a collection of agricultural equipment.

The Antikensammlung (Department of Antiquities), on the first floor, contains some notable examples of Greek and Roman architecture and sculpture.

Department of Antiquities

A particular attraction is the Pergamon Altar, one of the wonders of the ancient world. The altar, dedicated to Zeus and Athena (tutelary goddess of the city of Pergamon in Asia Minor), dates from about 180–160 B.C., and was brought to Berlin in 1902. Other important exhibits are examples of Hellenistic architecture from Priene, Magnesia and Miletus (gate of the Roman market in Miletus, 165 B.C.) and early Greek sculpture from Miletus, Samos, Naxos and Attica.

The Vorderasiatisches Museum (Western Asian Museum) is also on the first floor. Its 14 rooms give a comprehensive view of 4000 years of history, art and culture in Western Asia. It contains important examples of Neo-Babylonian architecture, and is the world's third largest collection of its kind, with material from the time of Nebuchadnezzar II (603–562 B.C.) – the monumental Ishtar Gate, the processional way and part of the façade of the Throne Room from Babylon. Other examples of monumental architecture from Western Asia are the mosaic wall (c. 3000 B.C.) and the brick façade (c. 1415 B.C.) from the Sanctuary of Eanna in Uruk; the gigantic figure of a bird from Tell Halaf (c. 900 B.C.); the Victory Stela of King Esarhaddon of Assyria (680–669 B.C.); and the large Lion Gate from the Citadel of Sinjerli.

Western Asian Museum

Smaller objects (small sculpture, cuneiform tablets, etc.) are displayed in the showcases.

The Islamisches Museum (Islamic Museum) on the second floor was established by Wilhelm von Bode in 1904. Its most valuable exhibit is the façade of the desert Castle of Mshatta in Jordan (8th c.), presented to the German Emperor by the Sultan of Turkey. Other important items are the early 17th c. room from Aleppo, a prayer-niche from the Maidan Mosque in Kashan, and Persian and Indian miniatures, carpets and woodcarving.

Islamic Museum

During the last war this part of the museum suffered heavy losses, and many of the exhibits had to be restored and reconstructed, including the left-hand tower of the Mshatta Castle (completed 1963).

The Ostasiatische Sammlung (East Asian Collection), also on the second floor, was established, again by Wilhelm von Bode, in 1907. It has a large collection of Chinese ceramics, covering a period of more than 4000 years, together with enamelwork, jade and lacquerware. Other items of interest include silks and embroidery of the 18th and 19th c. and Japanese coloured woodcuts, sword-guards and ceramics.

East Asian Collection

Platz der Akademie (Academy Square) B5

From Unter den Linden it is only 10-minutes walk to the Platz der Akademie. The square was originally known as the "Gendarmenmarkt" because a regiment of Gendarmerie had

Location
Berlin-Mitte

Platz der Akademie

Platz der Akademie (Gendarmenmarkt)

U-Bahn
Hausvogteiplatz

their guard-house and stables here from 1736 to 1782; it was given its present name in 1950, when the Academy of Sciences of the GDR celebrated its 250th anniversary. Before its destruction during the last war the Gendarmenmarkt was one of Berlin's finest squares. After many years of restoration work it is now slowly regaining its former appearance.

Schauspielhaus (Theatre)

The central feature of the square is the Schauspielhaus (Theatre), one of Schinkel's most notable buildings (1818–21), which occupies the site of the earlier National Theatre, burned down in 1817. The reliefs in the pediments and the figures of Muses on the roof are by Christian Friedrich Tieck; the pediment of the auditorium is by Christian Daniel Rauch.
In the autumn of 1984 the building was reopened as a concert hall (two auditoriums), with the exterior rebuilt in its original form.

German Cathedral

On the SW side of the square stands the Deutscher Dom (German Cathedral), built by Martin Grünberg between 1701 and 1708 for the Lutheran community of Berlin. The portico and domed tower were added by Carl Friedrich von Gontard during the reign of Frederick the Great. (At present being restored after war damage.)

French Cathedral

Opening times
Huguenot Museum:
Mon.–Fri. 10 a.m.–5 p.m.

The counterpart to the German Cathedral, on the N side of the square, is the Französischer Dom (French Cathedral), built by Louis Cayart and Quesnay in 1701–05 for the Huguenot community which had come to Berlin after Louis XIV's Revocation of the Edict of Nantes in 1685; the tower was added later by G. C. Unger, following C. F. von Gontard's design. After destruction during the war (1944) restoration of the church and tower was completed in 1983. The new basement of the church now houses the Huguenot Museum, with exhibits illustrating the history of the Huguenots in France and Prussia.

Postal Museum (Postmuseum)   B5

The Postal Museum was founded in 1872, and after suffering severe losses during the Second World War was reopened in 1948.

The museum developed out of an exhibition of plans and models established in the old General Post Office by Heinrich von Stephan. It now displays a rich collection of material illustrating the development of postal services and telecommunications, from the ancient Greek method of conveying messages by a form of telegraphy using torches to the modern Telex system. On the first floor is an exhibition of postage stamps.

Location
Leipziger Strasse/
Mauerstrasse,
Berlin-Mitte

Potsdam

Potsdam, once one of the most important Baroque towns of Germany, is most conveniently reached from the eastern part of the divided city by the two-decker trains running every hour between Potsdam and Drewitz; buses and cars have to make a long detour. (For visits to Potsdam see Practical Information – Sightseeing Tours.)

Potsdam lies in beautiful hilly country amid extensive areas of water – the River Havel, here taking on the dimensions of a lake, the Jungfernsee, the Tiefer See, the Griebnitzsee, the Templiner See.

The town first appears in the records in 993, in a charter granted by Otto III to the Monastery of Quedlinburg. There was a German castle on the site in the 12th c. In 1660 Potsdam became the residence of the Elector of Brandenburg. The Great Elector and Frederick the Great in particular left their mark on the town's architecture; but the town suffered heavy damage during the last war, and the new building does not make up for the loss of the old. The large Town Palace (Stadtschloss), built by Philipp de Chieze in 1660–82 and altered by Georg Wenzeslaus von Knobelsdorff in 1745–56, was totally destroyed, the ruins being finally pulled down in 1959–60. The Garnisonkirche (Garrison Church), with its three-storey tower by Philipp Gerlach and its famous carillon, was also destroyed.

Within the town itself the following historic features have survived or been rebuilt:

Notable buildings in this town

Dutch Quarter (Holländisches Viertel)
This part of the town, with gabled brick houses and a canal, was built between 1734 and 1752, on the orders of Frederick William I, to provide homes for settlers from the Low Countries in a style which would be familiar to them. The houses were later used for the quartering of troops.
Considerable restoration has been in progress since 1984.

Court Stables (Marstall)
This Baroque building, designed by Johann Arnold Nering and Georg Wenzeslaus von Knobelsdorff, was erected in 1746.

The Baroque former town hall (Rathaus)
(now the Hans Marchwitza Cultural Centre) The building, to a design by the Italian Andrea Palladio, was erected by Johann Boumann the Elder in 1753.

St Nicholas's Church (Nikolaikirche)

Opening times
Daily 10 a.m.–5 p.m.

St Nicholas's, rededicated in 1981 after restoration work lasting almost 35 years, is Potsdam's principal church and its dominant landmark, with a dome rising 53 m (175 ft) above the nave.

Built in 1831–37 on the site of an earlier Baroque church destroyed by fire in 1795, the church was designed by Karl Friedrich Schinkel as a domed church in Neo-Greek style; the four corner towers were added by F. A. Stüler and Ludwig Persius in 1843–50. Just before the First World War, in 1912–13, various minor alterations and renovations were carried out to improve the poor acoustics.

In April 1945 the church suffered what seemed irreparable damage. The dome, the organ-gallery and the paintings in the apse were destroyed, the portico was badly damaged, and the relief in the pediment was irreparably mutilated.

Work on clearing the rubble and making the church safe began in 1947, and by 1950 it could be used again for worship. By 1960 the dome had been rebuilt on the basis of the original plans of 1845, the copper required for this purpose being contributed by the churches of West Germany. By the early 1970s work on the exterior of the church was complete.

The interior of the church was altered from Schinkel's original plan so that it could be used not only for worship but as a community centre. The acoustics were still further improved, and the church is now used for concerts and recitals.

The French Church

The French Church was built in 1751–52 by J. Boumann the Elder to plans by Knobelsdorff as the central Baroque building. External reconstruction is to begin in 1986.

Sanssouci Palace (Schloss Sanssouci)

The great attraction of Potsdam lies not so much in the town itself as in the palace and park of Sanssouci.

Sanssouci Palace, built on six terraces on the summit of a vine-clad hill, was Frederick the Great's dream palace. Designed by Georg Wenzeslaus von Knobelsdorff on the basis of a sketch by the King himself and built in 1745–47, it is a single-storey building in Rococo style with a massive green central dome and yellow-washed walls, 97 m (318 ft) long and 12 m (39 ft) high. In this Palace of Sanssouci (Free of care) Frederick was able to give rein to the artistic interests which he had always pursued in spite of his father's opposition.

Exterior

On the garden front of the palace the cornice is supported by 35 massive caryatides. On the dome the name of Sanssouci is inscribed in letters of gold.

At the foot of the terraces (restored 1979–83) is the Parterre, an

Sanssouci Palace

ornamental basin surrounded by white marble statuary, with a high fountain jet in the middle.

The other side of the palace, the courtyard front, has a semicircular colonnade of 88 columns in two rows. In front of this, achieving a finely contrived effect of perspective, is the Ruinenberg (Hill of Ruins), an assemblage of ancient architectural elements.

The apartments open to the public (conducted tours only) include the Antechamber, the Marble Hall, various reception-rooms, the Concert Hall, workrooms and bedrooms, the panelled Library (not usually shown to visitors because of the danger of damage), the Little Gallery and a number of guest-rooms, including one occupied by Voltaire.

Interior
(open daily 9 a.m.–5 p.m.)

The rooms are decorated with reliefs, wall- and ceiling-paintings, rocaille-work, intarsia floors, carved doors and a profusion of gilding and mirrors.

Like the exterior, the interior of Sanssouci reflects Frederick's personal tastes: this is not a family residence but a palace designed to meet the requirements and satisfy the preferences of a single individual, the King.

Vestibule
The Vestibule is strictly ordered and disciplined. The columns here are more graceful than those in the colonnades.

Marble Hall
This is a room of cold magnificence, with columns and cornices, a huge dome and much carved decoration and sculpture.

119

Reception Room
An elegant room serving as reception-room, study or bedroom.

Music Room
An essentially private room, but splendidly decorated, with mural painting and mirrors, and gilded carving on musical themes. In the evenings the candles were lit in this room and the King played his flute accompanied by the other musicians. The scene is immortalised in a picture by Adolph von Menzel, "Flute Concerto in Sanssouci".

Library
This was the King's most private sanctum – a circular room with windows reaching up the full height of the walls, a star-patterned parquet floor, a massive chimneypiece, mirrors and a chandelier. The bookcases, of fine cedarwood and gilt bronze, fit into the decorative scheme – all with the same curving lines, topped by cartouches containing coats of arms, and with a glass-fronted case in the centre.

Park

The park of Sanssouci offers a series of ever-changing vistas: expanses of grass, clumps of trees, circular flowerbeds, terraces, a profusion of marble sculpture in single figures and groups (frequently on Greek mythological themes), obelisks, busts, vases and fountains, together with a number of gardens in the style of different countries, such as the Dutch Garden (1764–66, by Joachim Ludwig Heydert), the Sicilian Garden (1857, by Peter Joseph Lenné) and the Nordic Garden (1857, also by Lenné).

Eastern Pleasure Garden

In the Östlicher Lustgarten (Eastern Pleasure Garden) is the Bildergalerie (Picture Gallery), designed by Johann Gottfried Büring and built between 1755 and 1763 – a single-storey building with a central dome, long side wings and a Rococo façade which housed Frederick the Great's picture collection and still contains works by old masters.
The terrace in front of the Picture Gallery, with grotto-like walls, was laid out by J. L. Heydert in 1763–66.

Western Pleasure Garden

New Apartments
In the Westlicher Lustgarten (Western Pleasure Garden) are the Neue Kammern (New Apartments), originally built by Knobelsdorff in 1747 as an Orangery but altered by G. C. Unger in 1771–74 to provide accommodation for guests. The sculpture on the façade is by Friedrich Christian Glume, the allegorical figures along the garden front by 18th c. Italian sculptors.

Dutch Windmill
The Holländische Windmühle (Dutch Windmill) was built in 1790, replacing an earlier mill of 1739 associated with the legendary "miller of Sanssouci".
The familiar story is that the miller refused to give up this plot of land situated so close to Frederick's palace; and neither pleas nor threats of legal action, neither money not fair words, could move him. The story, we are told, may not be true, but it *could* have been true, for the King had promised "never to disturb the course of justice: in the courts the laws must speak and the King remain silent."

Chinese Teahouse
The Chinesisches Teehaus (Chinese Teahouse) was built by
Büring in 1754–57. The gilded sandstone sculpture is by
Johann Heymüller and Johann Benckert (*c.* 1757). Porcelain
exhibits.

Orangery
The Orangery, reached by way of the Sicilian and Nordic
Gardens, was built in 1851–57 by August Stüler and Ludwig
Hesse on the basis of designs by Ludwig Persius, following
Italian Renaissance models. The marble figures on the
balustrades of the loggias were carved by pupils of Christian
Daniel Rauch; some of the sculpture on the parapets of the
terraces is by Rauch himself.

The Jubiläumsterrasse (Jubilee Terrace) was laid out by
Emperor William II on the occasion of his jubilee (the 25th
anniversary of his accession).

Temple of Friendship
In the Rehgarten (Roedeer Garden) is the Freundschaftstempel
(Temple of Friendship), built by Carl von Gontard in 1768. The
marble reliefs on the eight Corinthian columns represent
famous pairs of friends of ancient times.

Roedeer Garden

New Palace
The Neues Palais (New Palace) was built in 1763–69 by
Büring, Heinrich Ludwig Manger and Gontard. A monumental
structure with a profusion of sculptural decoration, it was
designed to demonstrate the wealth of Prussia after the Seven
Years War. The dome, with its three Graces and crown,
symbolises the union of Prussia and the Arts. The balustrade on
the garden front is decorated with putti, trophies and vases
(19th c.). Palace Theatre; collection of old musical instruments.
The Communs (servants' quarters) to the rear of the palace,
which close the grand courtyard, were designed by Jean-
Laurent Legeay and Gontard.

Open 9 a.m.–5 p.m.

Ancient Temple, Dragon House, Belvedere
The Antiker Tempel (Ancient Temple) was built in 1768 by
Gontard, who took the Pantheon in Rome as his model. The
Drachenhaus (Dragon House), built in 1770, was modeled on
Sir William Chambers's Chinese Pagoda at Kew. The Belvedere
(by Unger, 1770–72) was based on a reconstruction of Nero's
Macellum in Rome.
The avenue which runs E to the Orangery was laid out in 1902.

Charlottenhof Palace, in the landscaped park, was built by
Schinkel in 1826 for Crown Prince Frederick William (later
Frederick William IV). It is in Neo-Classical style, in the manner
of an Italian villa.
The Roman Baths group of buildings (by Ludwig Persius,
1829–35) comprises the Italian-style Court Gardener's House,
the Roman Baths themselves, with an arcaded hall, the Bath
Attendants' House and the Pavilion, in the form of a Greek
temple. To one side is the Dairy Farm (Meierei; 1832), also in
the style of an Italian villa.
In the south of the park, west of Charlottenhof Palace is the
Hippodrome. For several years there stood here the monument
to Frederick II by Rauch (see Unter den Linden).

Landscaped park

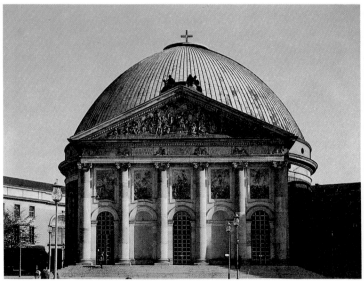

St Hedwig's Cathedral

Marly Garden

In the Marly Garden, laid out by Lenné about 1850, are the Peace Church (Friedenskirche) and Marly Palace. The church, built by Hesse and Ferdinand Arnim in 1845–54 on the basis of Frederick William IV's ideas and the plans of Persius, is a basilica imitating Roman models with a separate tower. The Mausoleum of Emperor Frederick III was built by Julius Raschdorf in 1892.

New Garden

The English-style Neuer Garten (New Garden) was laid out by Frederick William II on the W side of the Heiliger See (Sacred Lake) as a counterpart to Sanssouci.
The Marmorpalais (Marble Palace), built in 1787–90 by Gontard and Langhans, was the residence (until 1917) of the last Crown Prince. It now houses a Military Museum.
Near by is Cecilienhof Palace, now a hotel, which was built in 1913–16. The Potsdam Agreement between the victorious Allies was signed here in 1945.

Princesses' Palace (Prinzessinnenpalais)

See Operncafé

St Hedwig's Cathedral (St.-Hedwigs-Kathedrale)   B5

Location
Bebelplatz, Berlin-Mitte

The building of this Baroque cathedral, modeled on the Pantheon in Rome, began in 1747 (architect Jean-Laurent

View of the Cathedral, the Television Tower and the Palace of the Republic

Legeay). The money required to built it was collected in Roman Catholic countries by a Carmelite monk named Mecanati; the site was provided by Frederick the Great.

After the end of the Seven Years War building continued in 1772 under the direction of Johann Boumann the Elder, and the church was consecrated in November 1773. It was named St Hedwig's Cathedral after the wife of Duke Henry of Silesia, who was much revered in Silesia. (The conquest of Silesia by Frederick the Great had for the first time incorporated large Roman Catholic territories in Prussia.)

The church was destroyed by fire during the Second World War and was rebuilt between 1952 and 1963. The interior is modern (architect Hans Schwippert), but the original structure of the dome has been preserved.

The Cathedral is the seat of the Roman Catholic Bishop of Berlin.

U-Bahn
Hausvogteiplatz

Buses
9, 57, 78

St Mary's Church

See Marienkirche

St Nicholas's Church

See Nikolaikirche

Soviet Embassy (Sowjetische Botschaft)   B4/5

Location
Unter den Linden 63–65,
Berlin-Mitte

S-Bahn
Friedrichstrasse .

Bus
9

The Soviet Embassy occupies the site of the palace of Princess Amalie, built in 1734, which from 1832 was the residence of the Russian Ambassador. Tsar Nicholas I purchased the house and had it altered by Eduard Knoblauch in 1840–41. The building was destroyed during the Second World War.

After the war this was the first building in Unter den Linden to be rebuilt (by the Soviet architects Lbedinsky, Sikhert, Skuyin and Stryshevsky).

Immediately E of the Embassy are the offices of the Soviet travel agency and trade delegation.

Soviet Memorial

See Treptow Park

*Television Tower (Fernsehturm)   B5

Location
Alexanderplatz,
Berlin-Mitte

The Television Tower has become the new landmark and emblem of East Berlin. Statistics: height (with aerial) 365 m (1200 ft), concrete shaft 250 m (820 ft), weight of tower 26,000 tons, weight of sphere 4800 tons, observation terrace

Town Hall and Television Tower

for 200 people at 207 m (680 ft), diameter of base 32 m (105 ft), diameter of observation floor 24 m (80 ft), diameter of Tele-Café (accommodation for 200) 29 m (95 ft).

The tower was designed by Fritz Dieter and Günter Franke in co-operation with Swedish engineers. Work began in August 1965, and the tower was brought into operation in October 1969.

The ticket offices are on the upper floor of the hall at the foot of the tower. From there two high-speed lifts take visitors up to the observation floor (stay 30 minutes), from which there are panoramic views, extending in clear weather for anything up to 40 km (25 miles).

In the Tele-Café (stay 60 minutes) the tables and chairs are on a revolving ring which makes one complete turn every hour.

There is a special post office in the tower (open daily 9 a.m.–9 p.m.).

In the gardens between the Television Tower and the banks of the Spree and between the Town Hall and Karl-Liebknecht-Strasse is the Neptunbrunnen (Neptune Fountain), by Reinhold Begas (1891), depicting Neptune and his Court. The Berliners say that the ladies of Neptune's train are the only women in Berlin who can hold their tongue. The fountain originally stood between the Town Palace and the Court Stables.

From the Television Tower a flight of steps leads down to the gardens.

U-Bahn
Alexanderplatz

S-Bahn
Alexanderplatz

Opening times
April–Oct. daily 9 a.m.–11 p.m.
Nov.–March daily 8 a.m.–11 p.m. (every 2nd and 4th Mon. in the month open only 1 p.m.–11 p.m.)

Latest admission
Tele-cafe 10.00 p.m.
Observation floor 10.30 p.m.

Neptune Fountain

---

*Tierpark (Zoo)   B/C6

The Tierpark was originally the park of Friedrichsfelde Palace, laid out by Benjamin Raule for the Great Elector at the end of the 17th c. Opened in July 1955 (buildings and layout designed by Heinrich Dathe), the Tierpark has an area of 160 hectares (395 acres), 22·7 km (14 miles) of paths and 2·6 hectares (6½ acres) of lakes and ponds. It has a total of some 5000 animals in almost 1000 species.

A particular feature is the Alfred Brehm Animal House, a centrally situated glass hall with tropical vegetation, surrounded by cages and glass cases housing snakes, monitor lizards, large felines and some hundred species of birds.

The gardens are beautifully planted with rare species of plants, including 530 different orchids.

Conducted tours can be arranged for individual visitors or groups: apply in advance to the following address: DDR-1136 Berlin, Am Tierpark 125. A permit for photography costs 50 pfennigs a day. Visitors must not feed the animals.

Location
Friedrichsfelde

U-Bahn
Tierpark

Opening times
Summer: daily 7 a.m. to dusk; winter: daily 8 a.m. to dusk

Town Hall (Rathaus)   B5

Berlin's first Town Hall is believed to have stood in the Molkenmarkt (see entry) in the 13th c. From 1307 to 1442, when the towns of Cölln and Berlin were united, the Town Hall serving both towns stood by the Long Bridge (Lange Brücke).

Location
Rathausstrasse,
Berlin-Mitte

Later the Town Hall, with an open arcade where the municipal court sat, and a clock tower (attested at the beginning of the 15th c.), was in Königstrasse (later Rathausstrasse). After being damaged by fire the Town Hall was rebuilt and provided with a new court room and a torture chamber (in the basement). The place of execution was in the square in front of the arcade previously occupied by the court, until an Electoral Decree in 1694 moved it elsewhere – on account, as the decree phrased it, of the disturbance it caused to traffic.

By the middle of the 19th c. the deteriorating condition of the structure and lack of space made a new building necessary. This was designed by Hermann Friedrich Waesemann and built between 1861 and 1869 – a massive Neo-Renaissance building laid out round three inner courtyards with a tower 74 m (243 ft) high. The foundation-stone was laid in June 1861 in the presence of King William I and the first meeting of the Town Council was held at the end of 1865, although the building was not completed until late in 1869. The new Town Hall is the seat of the Chief Burgomaster and the municipal authorities of East Berlin.

The dominant feature of the Town Hall is the clock tower above the main entrance. It soon became known as the Red Town Hall, from the red brick of which it was built – and perhaps also on account of the democratic spirit shown by the municipal authorities even in the time of the Empire. Round the building at first-floor level extends the "Chronicle" (Chronik), a series of scenes from the history of Berlin (by O. Geyer, R. Schweinitz and A. Calandrelli).

In front of the Town Hall are two statues, the "Trümmerfrau" (a woman clearing rubble) and the "Aufbauhelfer" (a worker assisting in the reconstruction of Berlin).

The Rathauskeller (Town Hall Cellar) is a restaurant which serves Berlin specialities.

Treptow Park and Soviet Memorial   C5/6
(Treptower Park, Sowjetisches Ehrenmal)

The best starting-point for a visit to Treptow Park is the S-Bahn station, there is a long walk from the bus and tram termini and the park is not easily reached from the city centre by other forms of public transport. Treptow Park (area 230 hectares (570 acres)) was a popular place of recreation for the people of Berlin even before it formally became a municipal park. The park and the adjoining Plänterwald were laid out in the style of an English landscaped park in 1876–88 by the first municipal Superintendent of Parks, Gustav Meyer, a pupil of the great landscape-gardener Peter Joseph Lenné. The Berlin Industrial Exhibition was held in the park in 1896, when the Archenhold Observatory (see entry), to the right of the Puschkin-Allee, was built.

Coming from the S-Bahn station, we see on the left the River Spree, with the river port used by the Weisse Flotte (White Fleet), from which there are numerous boat services on the waterways of East Berlin, reaching as far afield as the Spree Forest. To the right, beyond a large expanse of grass, is the

Unter den Linden ▶

Soviet Memorial. On the left towards the River Spree lies the Rose Garden.

The area in front of the Zenner Restaurant (built in 1821–22 by C. F. Langhans) is the scene in alternate years of a large open-air exhibition by the Verband der Bildenden Künstler der DDR (Artists' Union), "Sculpture and Flowers".

Treptow Park merges imperceptibly into the Plänterwald.

Soviet Memorial

From the S-Bahn station it is 10 minutes' walk along the Puschkin-Allee to the Soviet Memorial, designed by the sculptor Evgeny V. Vuchetich and the architect Yakov B. Belopolsky and erected in 1947–49.

This is the central memorial to the Soviet soldiers who fell in the battle for Berlin in 1945. On the stone gateways at the entrances to the Memorial (in the road skirting Treptow Park and in the Puschkin-Allee) are the words, in Russian and German: "Eternal glory to the heroes who fell for the freedom and independence of the socialist homeland."

In the avenue leading to the entrance is a female figure, "Mutter Heimat" ("Mother Homeland"), carved from a 50-ton block of granite. A broad path lined by silver birches leads to the Ehrenhain (Grove of Honour), with two walls of red granite symbolising flags lowered in mourning, on the ends of which are bronze figures of kneeling Red Army men.

In the centre of the memorial, the burial-place of 5000 Soviet soldiers, are five stretches of lawn, with five stone bases bearing bronze wreaths; on each side of the grove are eight stone sarcophagi.

The central feature of the memorial is the Ehrenhügel (Hill of Honour), on which stands a cylindrical mausoleum bearing a huge figure of a Soviet soldier, 11·60 m (38 ft) high. On his left arm he holds a child, in his right hand the sword with which he has shattered the Nazi swastika.

A flight of steps leads up to a domed chamber under the statue, which weighs 70 tons. The interior of the mausoleum is

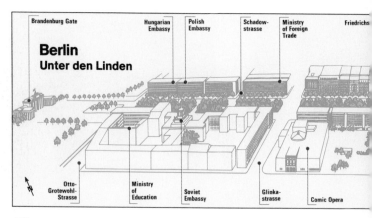

decorated with mosaics (by the Soviet painter Gorpenko) depicting representatives of the various Soviet Republics mourning their dead. On the ceiling is the Order of Victory of the Soviet Union.

The total length of the Memorial is 500 m (550 yds).

**Unter den Linden   B4/5

Unter den Linden ("Under the Lime-Trees") is a broad avenue running from Marx-Engels-Platz to the Brandenburg Gate (see entry). At No. 23 was the Gasthaus zur Sonne (Sun Inn), later the Russischer Hof, in which Goethe once stayed; at No. 24 was a house in which Heinrich Heine lived.

From 1573 there was a riding-track here, used by the Elector on his way to the Tiergarten to hunt. In 1647 the Great Elector caused six rows of nut trees and limes to be planted along the road, but when the road was surfaced in 1675 these were removed. The chronicles of Berlin record the various types of building which now began to be erected along the road – dwelling-houses, workshops, public buildings, palaces. To the N there grew up the district of Dorotheenstadt. The Friedrichstadt area to the S was developed between 1688 and 1692 to the design of J. J. Beer.

The first building of consequence in Unter den Linden was the Arsenal (see entry), and soon afterwards the Gendarmenmarkt, now the Platz der Akademie (see entry), was laid out. In 1734 the street, which had hitherto reached only as far as Schadowstrasse, was extended to the Pariser Platz. Frederick the Great then commissioned Georg Wenzeslaus von Knobelsdorff to design a street in the grand manner which should be the cultural centre of Berlin; but Knobelsdorff soon fell into disfavour, and was able to complete only the Opera House (see entry). Other architects continued the work: St Hedwig's Cathedral (see entry) was designed by Jean-Laurent Legeay,

Location
Berlin-Mitte

S-Bahn
Friedrichstrasse

Buses
9, 57

First major buildings

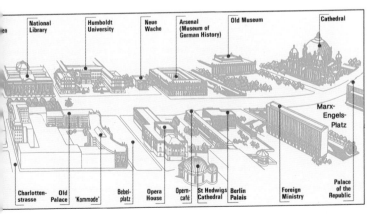

129

J. G. Büring and Johann Boumann the Elder, the Old Library by G. C. Unger. In 1789–91 the street was given a worthy terminal point in the Brandenburg Gate (see entry), designed by Langhans. In 1816–18 the Neue Wache (see entry) was built by K. F. Schinkel, who was also responsible for the Palace Bridge, now the Marx-Engels Bridge.

Monument to Freiherr vom Stein

Between the Marx-Engels Bridge and the Berlin Palace (see entry), at the end of the Foreign Ministry, is a bronze statue of the Prussian reformer and statesman Freiherr vom Stein, re-erected here in March 1981. The statue (1860–64) is the finest work of the Berlin sculptor Hermann Schievelbein (1817–67), one of the younger members of the Rauch school.

The statue, 3·30 m (11 ft) high, shows Freiherr vom Stein (1757–1831), wearing the Order of the Black Eagle, leaning on a stick held in his left hand and holding up his right hand in a gesture of command.

The base, 4·50 m (15 ft) high, was left unfinished on Schievelbein's death and was completed by Hugo Hagen. At the corners are four life-size statues symbolising Stein's virtues – patriotism, energy, honesty and piety. One of the figures points to the "Monumenta Germaniae Historica", a collection of medieval sources on German history which was initiated by him.

Four large bronze reliefs on the base depict mythological scenes: Hope promising Borussia (Prussia) a glorious future; the spirit of sacrifice of the Prussian people; Borussia leading her children into battle; the victors crowned with garlands.

A narrow frieze below these scenes shows events in the life of Freiherr vom Stein: the reform of Prussian administration, 1807–08; abolition of serfdom; raising of the Landwehr (National Militia); Tsar Alexander visiting Stein; the Allied entry into Leipzig; Stein vowing to pursue the enemy to Paris; opening of the first Diet of Westphalia; municipal reorganisation, 1808.

The monument, originally erected in 1870, suffered severe damage during the Second World War. It was removed from its original site in 1969, restored and re-erected in its present position in 1981, on the 150th anniversary of Freiherr vom Stein's death.

Going west from the Marx-Engels Bridge in the direction of the Brandenburg Gate, we see on the right the Arsenal and beyond this the Neue Wache, now a memorial to the victims of Fascism and militarism. Beyond this again is a clump of chestnut trees, with the Academy of Singing, now the Maxim Gorki Theatre, adjoining which is the House of German-Soviet Friendship.

Statue of Frederick the Great

The 14 m (46 ft) high statue, by Christian Daniel Rauch (1851), was re-erected here in 1980. The King is depicted riding on his favourite horse, Condé, wearing his coronation robes, three-cornered hat and topboots and holding a stick. On four large tablets on the lower part of the base are the names of 60 of the leading men of Frederick's reign; above these are life-size figures of generals, and at the corners cavalry commanders; and above these again are bas-reliefs of scenes from Frederick's life and allegorical figures.

Other buildings and statues

Opposite the Neue Wache, in Oberwallstrasse, is the Crown Prince's Palace (see Berlin Palace), built by Frederick William I for his son, and at the south-west corner is the Princesses'

Palace (see Operncafé), once the residence of Frederick William III's three daughters. Both palaces were completely destroyed during the Second World War and rebuilt after the war.

In a small public garden are statues of Generals Blücher, Gneisenau, Scharnhorst and Yorck (from C. D. Rauch's workshop).

On the same side of the street are the Opera House (see entry), also burned down and rebuilt, and, behind it in the south-east corner of Bebelplatz, St Hedwig's Cathedral (see entry) and the rebuilt Emperor William Palace, popularly known as the "Kommode" (Chest of Drawers), which is now part of the Humboldt University (see entry). Adjoining this there formerly stood the Dutch Palace, which was completely destroyed during the last war. Its site is now occupied by the New Governor's House, the façade of which has sculptural decoration from the old Commandant's House at the corner of Rathausstrasse and Judenstrasse.

On the opposite side of the street is the extensive range of buildings occupied by the Humboldt University (see entry), with rare ginkgo trees in the front gardens and statues of Alexander and Wilhelm von Humboldt in front of the main entrance. Adjoining are the National Library and departments of the Academy of Sciences (see entries). At the south-west corner of the intersection of Unter den Linden with Friedrich-strasse there once stood the famous old Café Bauer; its site is now occupied by the large Lindencorso Restaurant.

At the north-east corner, on the site of the old Hotel and Café Victoria (later the Café König), is the eight-storey Unter den Linden Hotel. The Haus der Schweiz (House of Switzerland) opposite it is one of the few buildings in the street to survive the war almost unscathed. To the south of the intersection are the administrative offices of the Comic Opera.

The upper part of Unter den Linden is lined by office buildings. From here there is a good view of the Brandenburg Gate and the Pariser Platz, a closed area surrounded by barriers. At the SE corner of the square there formerly stood the famous Adlon Hotel, part of which still survives and is run as a hotel.

Western Asian Museum (Vorderasiatisches Museum)

See Pergamon Museum

Zoo

See Tierpark

Practical Information

Access

By car

Visitors travelling in their own car can reach West Berlin by the following frontier crossings and roads:
- Gudow/Zarrentin, then motorway E15 and road 5 to Staaken/Heerstrasse (West Berlin).
- Helmstedt/Marienborn, then motorway to Drewitz/Dreilinden (West Berlin).
- Herleshausen/Wartha, then motorway to Drewitz/Dreilinden (West Berlin).
- Rudolphstein/Hirschberg, then motorway to Drewitz/Dreilinden (West Berlin).

Driving in the GDR

Visitors may choose any one of the four permitted routes, and need not return by the same route.

The entry points are open night and day.

Motorists with a transit visa are obliged to follow these specific routes, marked with the word "Transit" on a yellow board. Travellers should be careful to avoid an incautious act or behaviour which might be interpreted as a breach of the law of the GDR. Some activities which may be legal in the UK are regarded as offences in the GDR. There are severe penalties for activities which are regarded as directed against the security of the State – for example if someone is thought to be conducting propaganda against the Government.

The following is a summary of the most important transit routes regulations:
(a) Newspapers, leaflets, etc. may not be distributed nor accepted.
(b) Persons such as hitch-hikers may not be picked up.
(c) Transit routes should not be left, except in cases of emergency (accident or illness) and by arrangement with the GDR authorities.
(d) The road traffic regulations must be strictly observed, e.g. speed limits.

Any infringement against the "Transit Agreement" is a breach of the GDR Law. The punishment can vary from a warning or a fine to imprisonment.

Drivers must carry their driving licence and car papers, as well as a valid passport.

Speed limits are 100 km p.h. (62 m.p.h.) on motorways, 80 km p.h. (50 m.p.h.) on ordinary roads and 50 km p.h. (31 m.p.h.) in built-up areas. Seat-belts must be worn. The regulations are strictly enforced.

It is recommended that visiting motorists carry a first-aid kit, fire extinguisher and a set of replacement bulbs in their vehicle.

Cars may stop only in marked parking-places.

Petrol can be obtained at Inter-Tankstellen (petrol stations). Payment must be made in West German marks (DM) or other freely convertible currency.

Breakdown assistance

In case of breakdown help can be obtained from mobile patrols, which can be summoned on the motorway telephones. The following information should be given: location of the car, registration number, make and type, address of owner, likely cause of breakdown. The central accident report centre of the district can also be contacted on the motorway telephones.

There are regular bus services to West Berlin from the Federal Republic including services from Altenau, Bad Sachsa. Brunswick, Bremen, Düsseldorf, Flensburg, Frankfurt/Main, Hamburg, Hanover, Kiel, Lübeck, Munich, Nuremberg, Warmensteinach and Wolfsburg. Buses from West Berlin to West Germany depart from the Bus Station at the Radio Tower. The baggage allowance is 50 kg (110 lb).
Many travel firms offer package trips to Berlin (week-end or longer).

By bus

Visitors flying to West Berlin Tegel Airport are not subject to GDR controls. Passport and personal controls are carried out at the airports.
There are direct flights to West Berlin from London, Manchester and Glasgow and from various West German airports. Flights to Berlin from West Germany are subsidised and are, therefore, cheaper than other domestic flights.

By air

Trains from West Germany use the Büchen/Schwanheide, Helmstedt/Marienborn, Bebra/Gerstungen, Ludwigsstadt/Probstzella and Hof/Gutenfürst frontier crossings and arrive at the Zoo Station, the only long-distance station in West Berlin. Most trains have restaurant cars and sleeping-cars and couchettes for night travel. Passport control and the issue of visas take place during the journey. There are no baggage controls. The German Federal Railways (Bundesbahn) offer reasonably priced trips to Berlin, including week-end trips and special programmes.

By rail

Airlines

British Airways, Tegel Airport and Europa-Center; tel. 69 10 21.
Pan Am, Tegel Airport and Europa-Center; tel. 88 10 11.

West Berlin

Aeroflot, Unter den Linden 51–53; tel. 2 29 28 33.
British Airways, c/o Interflug, Alexanderplatz; tel. 5 55 72 22.
Interflug, Schönefeld Airport; tel. 67 20.

East Berlin

Airports

West Berlin has three airports, Berlin-Tempelhof, Gatow and Berlin-Tegel. Since 1975 Tempelhof has been closed to civil traffic, which is handled by Tegel.
Gatow is a British military airport.

West Berlin

Berlin-Schönefeld is the central airport of the German Democratic Republic.

East Berlin

Antiques

Anyone interested in antiques, whether in furniture, glassware, clocks pewter, porcelain, pictures or jewellery, will find just about every facility in Berlin, from the well-known and expensive shops to the little junks dealers. Most of the shops are located in the Kurfürstendamm and nearby streets (especially in Schlüterstrasse and Fasanenstrasse), as well as in Keithstrasse (near Wittenbergplatz) and in Eisenachstrasse (Schöneberg). Also of great interest are the "flea markets" in the former Nollendorfplatz U-Bahn station and in the "Ku'damm Karree". Unusual objects can be found in the junk market at the "Tempodrom" between the former Anhalter Station and Potsdamer Platz.

Flea markets   See Markets
Junk markets

Banks

Before the Second World War the old banking quarter of Berlin was around Jägerstrasse and Behrenstrasse (now in East Berlin). Since the war a new banking district has grown up in the Hardenbergstrasse district of West Berlin.

Opening times
Mon. and Wed. 9 a.m.–3 p.m.; Tue. and Thu. 9 a.m.–6 p.m.; Fri. 9 a.m.–1 p.m. Longer and extra opening times are shown in brackets in the following list. For exchange offices, see below.

West Berlin
Berliner Bank, Tegel Airport
(open daily 8 a.m.–10 p.m.)

Berliner Bank, City Service, Kurfürstendamm 18–24
(open Mon.–Fri. 9 a.m.–6.30 p.m. Sat. 9.30 a.m.–1.30 p.m.)

Berliner Commerzbank, in Wertheim's department store, Kurfürstendamm 230
(open Mon.– Fri. 10.30 a.m.–6 p.m., Sat. 10.30 a.m.–2 or 6 p.m.)

Bank für Handel und Industrie, Kurfürstendamm 26a
(open Sat. 10 a.m.–1 p.m.)
in KaDeWe, Tauentzienstr. 21
(open Mon.–Fri. 10 a.m.–6.30 p.m., Sat. 10 a.m.–2 or 6 p.m.)

Sparkasse, at Emperor William Memorial Church
(open Sat. 10 a.m.–1 p.m.)

Exchange offices
Zoo Station
(open Mon.–Sat. 8 a.m.–9 p.m., Sun. and pub. holidays 10 a.m.–6 p.m.)
Aschingerhaus, Joachimstaler Strasse 1
(open Mon.–Fri. 7.30 a.m.–9.30 p.m., Sat 7.30 a.m.–6 p.m.)

Changing money at post offices
See Postal services

Banks in East Berlin
Deutsche Handelsbank, Behrenstrasse 22
Berliner Stadtkontor-Ost
Behrenstrasse 39
Sparkasse der Stadt Berlin, Alexanderplatz 2
Staatsbank der DDR, Charlottenstrasse 32/33

Boat trips

In addition to the large numbers of pleasure craft (sailing-boats, rowing-boats, canoes) on the River Havel and its lakes there are also numerous excursion ships run by various Berlin companies and agencies, often with bands to provide a musical accompaniment.
The following companies run special moonlight and dance excursions as well as the usual round trips.

Reederei H. Riedel,
Planufer 78; tel. 6 91 37 82 and 6 93 46 46
Reederei Triebler
Johannastrasse 24; tel. 3 31 54 14

Stern- und Kreisschiffahrt,
Sachtlebenstrasse 60; tel. 8 100040

Reederei B. Winkler,
Levetzowstrasse 16; tel. 3 91 70 10

See also Sightseeing Tours.

Bookshops (a selection)

Elwert und Meurer,
Hauptstrasse 101

Galerie 2000,
Knesebeckstrasse 56
Art books, art catalogues, books of photography

Heinrich Heine Buchhandlung,
Zoo S-Bahn Station
Second-hand department

Herder'sche Buchhandlung,
Kurfürstendamm 69

Kiepert,
Hardenbergstrasse 4

Schikowski,
Motzstrasse 30
Astrology and occultism

Schropp'sche Landkartenanstalt,
Potsdamer Strasse 100
Maps

Düwal,   Secondhand bookshops
Schlüterstrasse 17
Books on many subjects, graphic art

Henning,
Motzstrasse 25
Books on many subjects, prints, periodicals

Practical Information

Koch,
Kurfürstendamm 216 (upper ground floor)
Old town views and maps

Wegner,
Martin-Luther-Strasse 113
Books on Berlin, the theatre, cinema

Cafés and Pâtisseries

The following is a selection of cafés on or near the Kurfürstendamm, Berlin's main shopping area; but there are also large numbers of cafés in other areas including Wilmersdorf, Steglitz and Schöneberg.

Cafés and Pâtisseries

Bristol, Kurfürstendamm 35
Café Adlon, Kurfürstendamm 69
Café des Westens, Ku'dammeck
Café Pientka, Kurfürstendamm 14
Gloria, Kurfürstendamm 12
Huthmacher, Hardenbergstr. 29d
I-Punkt, Europa Centre
Kempinski Eck, Kurfürstendamm 27
Kranzler, Kurfürstendamm 18
Krumme, Joachimstaler Strasse 41
Café Leysieffer, Kurfürstendamm 218
Mohring, Kurfürstendamm 163, 213 and 234

Café Kranzler, Kurfürstendamm

Tiffany's (tropical plants), Europa Centre
Wagenknecht, Olivaer Platz 18

Café Bleibtreu, Bleibtreustr. 45
Café Huthmacher, Hardenbergstr. 29d
Café Kranzler, Kurfürstendamm 18
Café Mohring, Kurfürstendamm 213
Café Pientka, Kurfürstendamm 14
Café Wagenknecht, Olivaer Platz 18

Camping

Deutscher Camping Club, Geisbergstrasse 11; tel. 24 60 71   Camping Club

Campingplatz Kohlhasenbrück,   Camping sites
Neue Kreisstrasse/Stubenrauchstrasse; tel. 8 05 17 37
Open 1 April–30 September

Campingplatz Kladow,
Krampnitzer Weg 111–117; tel. 3 65 27 97
Open throughout the year

Campingplatz Dreilinden,
Albrechts-Teerofen-Strasse 1–39; tel. 8 05 12 01
Open throughout the year

Campingplatz Haselhorst,
Pulvermühlenweg; tel. 3 34 59 55
Open throughout the year

Car rental (Autoverleih)

Avis,   West Berlin
Budapester Strasse 43; tel. 2 61 18 81
Tegel Airport; tel. 41 01 31 48

Europcar,
Kurfürstenstrasse 101; tel. 2 13 70 97;
Tegel Airport; tel. 41 01 33 23

Hertz,
Budapester Strasse 39; tel. 2 61 10 53;
Tegel Airport; tel. 41 01 33 15

InterRent,
Kurfürstendamm 178; tel. 8 81 80 93;
Tegel Airport; tel. 41 01 33 68

Chemists (Apotheken)

See Pharmacies

Churches (Kirchen)

West Berlin	Berlin has more than 200 Protestant and some 80 Roman Catholic churches. In addition there are a small number of synagogues and a Jewish community centre as well as the churches of various foreign communities.
	Times of services are given on a leaflet included with the newspapers on Fridays.
Protestant churches	Nicolaikirche, Reformationsplatz, Spandau
	The church, dedicated to St Nicholas of Myra, probably dates from the 14th–15th c. It was badly damaged by incendiary bombs in October 1944, but was restored soon after the war (architects Fangmeyer and Hahn).
	Luisenkirche, Gerkeplatz, Charlottenburg
	The church in its present form dates from 1823 (architects Schinkel and Gerlach).
	Emperor William Memorial Church (see A to Z)
Roman Catholic churches	Maria Regina Martyrum (see A to Z)
	St Canisius, Charlottenburg
Synagogues	Jewish Community House (see A to Z)
	Fraenkelufer 10–16
	Pestalozzistrasse 14–15
	Joachimstaler Strasse 13
	Iranische Strasse 3
Foreign communities	American Church, McNair Chapel, Lichterfelde-Süd
	British Church, Preussenallee, Westend
	French Reformed Church, Joachim-Friedrich-Strasse 4, Halensee
Churches in East Berlin	Churches in the centre of the city:
Protestant churches	Marienkirche (see A to Z)
	Cathedral (see A to Z)
Roman Catholic church	St Hedwig's Cathedral (see A to Z)

Oranienburger Strasse

Ryhestrasse 53

See under Music

Cinemas (Kinos)

West Berlin has more than 100 cinemas. To find out what is on, consult the periodicals "tip" and "zitty", the newspapers and the advertisement columns in the streets.

West Berlin

Department stores (Kaufhäuser)

Europa-Center, Breitscheidplatz
Forum Steglitz, Schlosstrasse 1
Ku-Damm Eck, Kurfürstendamm/Joachimstaler Strasse
KaDeWe (Kaufhaus des Westens), Wittenbergplatz
Wertheim, Kurfürstendamm 231

East Berlin, Entry into

Information and advice can be obtained from the Senator for Internal Affairs. Central Advice Office for East–West Traffic, Berlin 31, Fehrbelliner Platz 2 (Mon. Tue. and Fri. 9 a.m.–noon, Thu. 4–6 p.m.; tel. 867 1).

DDR currency may not be imported. All visitors over 15 years of age must change 25 DM per person and per day (7·5 DM for children over the age of six). Retirees must change 15 DM for a visit lasting one day.
Changing more than the minimum amount is permitted, but exchange of East German currency back into DM is only allowed for sums above the compulsory minimum. East German currency may not be taken into West Berlin.
West German and other Western currencies can be taken in without limit, but must be declared.

Currency

Visitors must not take into East Berlin any newspapers, periodicals or books.

Printed matter

The entry points for day visitors travelling on foot or by car are at Bornholmer Strasse and Prinzenstrasse/Heinrich-Heine-Strasse, for those travelling by S-Bahn or U-Bahn the Friedrichstrasse Station. They are open from 7 a.m. to midnight (no entry after 8 p.m.). The other entry points in Berlin may not be used by West Germans.

Entry points for West Germans

The entry points for day visitors are at Friedrichstrasse Station and Checkpoint Charlie (at Kochstrasse U-Bahn Station).
Visitors must have valid travel documents (passport, etc.); motorists must have their driving licence and the car papers.
It is important to have an up-to-date passport photograph, since visitors wearing a beard or spectacles are sometimes

Entry points for foreigners

139

Practical Information

turned back if their photograph does not tally with their appearance.

Getting to the entry points

To Bornholmer Strasse: from Kurfürstendamm U-Bahn Station to Osloer Strasse Station, then bus 89.

To Prinzenstrasse/Heinrich-Heine-Strasse: from Zoo U-Bahn Station to Kottbbusser Tor, then change for Moritzplatz; or bus 29 from Kurfürstendamm to Moritzplatz.

To Friedrichstrasse: S-Bahn from Zoo Station; bus 29 from Kurfürstendamm.

To Checkpoint Charlie: U-Bahn from Zoo to Hallesches, then change for Kochstrasse.

Events

January/February	International Green Week (agricultural and food show)
February/March	International Film Festival (Berlinale)
March	International Tourism Exchange Boat, Sport and Leisure Show
April	Day of the Open door Blossom Festival

Trotting Derby

Free Berlin Art Exhibition
Wasser Berlin (specialist exhibition for water undertakings)

Drama Meeting	May
May Days of Neukölln	
Whitsun: International Tennis Tournament at "Rot-Weiss" in the Grunewald	
Parade of the Allies along the Strasse des 17 Juni	May/June
Horizonte (Berlin Festival)	May/July
German-French Festival	June/July
German-American Festival	
Bach Days	
Jazz in the Garden	
Serenade concerts in Charlottenburg Palace	
International Summer Festival	June/August
Kreuzberg Festival	August/September
International Radio Show (alternate years, next 1987, etc.)	
British Berlin Tattoo	
Overseas Import Fair, "Partners in Progress" (alternate years next 1987, etc.)	September/October
bautec Berlin (old, new and civic building)	
Berlin Festival	
Great art exhibitions	
German Riding Tournament (alternate years)	
October Festival at Radio Tower	
German Trotting Derby	
AAA Berlin (Auto, Avus Attraktionen; not every year)	
Kulinaria Berlin (restaurant and food show)	October/November
Six Day Race	
SURTEC (technical exhibition)	
International Book Fair	November
Bock Beer Festival	
Berlin Jazz Days	
International Riding and Jumping Tournament	
Antiqua (antique fair)	December
Christmas Fair at Radio Tower	
Festival of the Sporting Press	
New Year Festival at the Gedächtniskirche	

Galleries (selection)

Information can be obtained from the Interessengemeinschaft
Berliner Kunsthändler e.V. Berlin-Wilmersdorf, Ludwigkirch-
strasse 11a, tel. 8 83 26 43

André-Anselm Dreher, Pfalzburger Strasse 80   Galleries in West Berlin
Contemporary art

Gerda Bassenge, Fasanenstrasse 73
Art gallery, urban pictures

Practical Information

DAAD, Kurfürstenstrasse 58
DAAD art programme

Dahlem-Dorf, Königin-Luise Strasse 48
Pictures, drawings, ceramics

Galerie des Lichts, Goethestrasse 81
Glass work

Galerie Kunsthandwerk Berlin
Pariser Strasse 12

Gärtner, Uhlandstrasse 20
Berlin subjects, pictures, graphic art, engravings

Werner Kunze, Giesebrechtstrasse 3
Early avant-garde, Art Deco, Object Art

Ladengalerie, Kurfürstendamm 64
Work by young Berlin sculptors

Ludwig Lange, Wielandstrasse 26
19th and 20th c. graphic art and sculpture

Majakowski, Kurfürstendamm 72
Graphic art, paintings, sculpture

Milan, Pfalzburger Strasse 76
Naïve and realistic painting

Nierendorf, Hardenbergstrasse 19
Classic Modernism, Expressionism, New Functionalism

Pels-Leusden, Kurfürstendamm 58
Classic Modernism to the present day

Petersen, Pestalozzistrasse 106
Pictures

Poll, Lützowplatz 7
Berlin Realists

Schüler, Kurfürstendamm 51
Contemporary art

Selbsthilfe Berliner Kunstler e.V., Wilhelm-Hauff Strasse 16
Community exhibitions

Westphal, Fasanenstrasse 68
Paintings

Brigitte Wölffer, Kurfürstendamm 206
Naïve painting

Galleries in East Berlin

Am Prater, Kastenienallee 100

Am Weidendamm, Friedrichstrasse

Arkade und Studiogalerie, Strausberger Platz 3–4

Ausstellungszentrum am Fernsehturm (exhibition centre) at the Television Tower)

Galerie im Turm, Frankfurter Tor 1

Kleine Kulturbund-Galerie, Zu den Sieben Raben 14

Mitte, Reinhardtstrasse 10

Neue Berliner Galerie, in the Old Museum

Neuer Marstall, in Marx-Engels-Platz 7

Skarabäus, Frankfurter Allee 80

Sophienstrasse, Sophienstrasse 8

Unter den Linden, Unter den Linden 62–68

Highways (Autobahnen)

About 44 km (28 miles) of the West Berlin highway network (including sections of the inner beltway) have been completed. The highway to West Germany (leaving the city in the direction of Wannsee) runs to the Dreilinden/Drewitz frontier crossing point.

Hotels

A list of all hotels in West Berlin can be obtained from the Tourist Office (Verkehrsamt), Europa Centre, Berlin 30 and its branches.
b=number of beds; SB=swimming bath

West Berlin

Alsterhof Ringhotel Berlin, Augsburger Strasse 5, Berlin 30, 250 b, (SB, Alsterstuben Restaurant)
Am Zoo, Kurfürstendamm 25, Berlin 15, 200 b.
Astoria am Bahnhof Zoo, Fasanenstr. 2, Berlin 12, 52 b.
Berlin, Kurfürstendamm 62, Berlin 30, 430 b, (Berlin Grill Restaurant)
Berlin Ambassador, Bayreuther Strasse 42–43, Berlin 30, 198 b (SB, Conti Fischstuben Restaurant)
Berlin Excelsior, Hardenbergstrasse 14, Berlin 12, 603 b.
Berlin Penta Hotel, Nürnberger Strasse 65, Berlin 30, 850 b (SB)
Bogotá, Schlüterstrasse 45, Berlin 15, 250 b.
Bremen, Bleibtreustrasse 25, Berlin 15, 72 b.
*Bristol Hotel Kempinski, Kurfürstendamm 27, Berlin 15, 645 b. (SB, Kempinski Grill Restaurant)
CC-City Castle, Kurfürstendamm 160, 100 b.
Eurotel Arosa, Liezenburger Strasse 79, Berlin 15, 147 b (SB, Walliser Stuben Restaurant) and Eurotel Arosa Aparthotel (no rest.), Liezenburger Strasse 82–84, Berlin 15, 173 b.
Franke, Albrecht-Achilles Strasse 57, Berlin 31, 100 b (SB).

Near Kurfürstendamm and Zoo Station

Practical Information

Hamburg, Landgrafenstrasse 4, Berlin 30, 330 b.
Hecker's Deele, Grolmanstrasse 35, Berlin 12, 120 b.
*Inter-Continental Berlin, Budapester Strasse 2, Berlin 30, 1150 b (SB, Zum Hugenotten Restaurant)
Meineke, Meinekestrasse 10, Berlin 15, 150 b.
Mondial, Kurfürstendamm 47, Berlin 30, 125 b (rooms for handicapped)
Palace, in Europa Centre, Budapester Strasse 42, Berlin 30, 250 b (grill restaurant)
President, An der Urania 16, Berlin 30, 123 b.
Residenz (no rest.), Meinekestrasse 9, Berlin 15, 114 b.
Savigny (no rest.), Brandenburgische Strasse 21, Berlin 31, 100 b.
Savoy, Fasenenstrasse 9, Berlin 12, 200 b.
Schweizerhof, Budapester Strasse 21, Berlin 30, 876 b) (SB; Schweizerhof Grill Restaurant).
*Steigenberger Berlin, Los Angeles Platz 1, Berlin 30, 600 b (SB, Park Restaurant)
Sylter Hof, Kurfürstendamm 116, Berlin 30, 220 b.

Charlottenburg

Am Studio (no rest.), Kaiserdamm 80–81, Berlin 19, 117 b.
Apartment Hotel Heerstrasse, Heerstrasse 80, Berlin 19, 70 b. (SB)
Econotel, Sömmeringstrasse 24, Berlin 10, 358 b.
Ibis, Messedamm 10, Berlin 19, 257 b.
Seehof, Lietzensee-Ufer 11, Berlin 19, 120 b. (SB, lakeside terrace)

Dahlem

Apartment-Hotel Sylvia, Warnemünder Strasse 19, Berlin 33, 33 b. (SB)

Grunewald

Belvedere, Seebergsteig 4, Berlin 33, 31 b.
Service area and Motel Grunewald, Kronprinzessinnenweg 120, Berlin 38, 74 b.
Schlosshotel Gehrhus, Brahmsstrasse 4–10, Berlin 33, 50 b.

Kreuzberg

Hervis Hotel International, Stresemannstrasse 97, Berlin 61, 140 b.

Siemensstadt

Novotel Berlin-Siemensstadt, Ohmstrasse 4–6, Berlin 13, 238 b. (SB)

Steglitz

Steglitz International, Albrechtstrasse 2, Berlin 41, 429 b.

Wilmersdorf

Berlin Crest Motor Hotel, Guntzelstrasse 14, Berlin 31, 220 b.

Hotels in East Berlin

Airport Hotel, Berlin-Schönefeld, 106 b.
Berolina, Karl-Marx-Allee 31, 607 b.
*Metropole, Friedrichstrasse 150–153, 700 b. (SB)
Newa, Invalidenstrasse 115, 109 b.
*Palasthotel, Karl-Liebknecht Strasse, 1006 b. (SB, Jade Restaurant)
Stadt Berlin, Alexanderplatz, 1908 b. (Panorama Restaurant on 37th floor)
Unter den Linden, Unter den Linden 14, 427 b.

Information

Verkehrsamt Berlin (Tourist Office),
Europa-Center (entrance Budapester Strasse),
tel. 2 12 34 and 2 62 60 31
Open 7.30 a.m.–10.30 p.m.

Verkehrsamt (Tourist Office),
Tegel Airport,
tel. 41 01 31 45
Open 8 a.m.–10.30 p.m.

Informationszentrum Berlin,
Hardenbergstrasse 20 (second floor),
tel. 3 10 04–0
Open Mon.–Fri. 8 a.m.–7 p.m., Sat. 8 a.m.–4 p.m.
Information and literature on political situation of Berlin

Kulturinformation,
Budapester Strasse 48,
tel. 25 48 90
Open Mon.–Fri. midday–6 p.m.
Information on Berlin Festivals

VEB Reisebüro der DDR
Haus des Reisens
Alexanderplatz 5
Tel. 2154402/03
Open Mon.–Fri. 8 a.m.–8 p.m.
Sat. and Sun. 9 a.m.–6 p.m.

West Berlin

Information in East Berlin

Libraries (Bibliotheken)

To borrow books a personal identity document (passport, etc.)
must be produced.

American Memorial Library
(see A to Z)

West Berlin

Art Library
(see A to Z)

Library of Free University of Berlin,
Henry-Ford-Bau, Garystrasse 39
(see A to Z, Free University of Berlin)

Library of University of Technology,
Strasse des 17 Juni 135

National Archives
(see A to Z)

National Library
(see A to Z)

Practical Information

Libraries in East Berlin

National Library
(see A to Z)

Council Library (Ratsbibliothek),
Marx-Engels-Platz 6–7

Municipal Library (Stadtbibliothek),
Breite Strasse 32–34

University Library (Universitätsbibliothek),
Clara Zetkin Strasse 27

Lost property offices (Fundbüros)

West Berlin

Fundbüro der Polizei,
Tempelhofer Damm 1; tel. 69 91

Fundbüro der Berliner Verkehrs-Betriebe (BVG),
Potsdamer Strasse 184; tel. 2 16 14 13
Objects lost on municipal transport services

Lost property offices in
East Berlin

Fundbüro der Deutschen Reichsbahn,
Marx-Engels-Platz, S-Bahn-Bogen 14. Tel. 4921671
Objects lost on trains (including S-Bahn)

Zentrales Fundbüro,
Wilhelm-Pieck-Strasse 164. Tel. 2829403
Objects lost on municipal transport services

Markets (Märkte)

Berlin has almost 70 weekly markets, 9 covered markets and
very many junk markets to tempt the visitor. It is here that you
get to know the Berliners; each market has its individual
features. Of the many weekly markets two especially should be
mentioned:

Weekly markets

Winterfeldplatz in Schöneberg
The largest weekly market in Berlin
Wed. and Sat. 8 a.m.–1 p.m.

Maybachufer in Neukölln
Turkish market
Tue. and Fri. noon–6.30 p.m.
Especially interesting on Friday afternoon

Flea markets

Ku'damm Karree,
Kurfürstendamm 207
Wed.–Fri. 3–10 p.m., Sat. and Sun. noon–10 p.m.

Nollendorfplatz U-Bahn Station
Daily, except Tue. 11 a.m.–7 p.m.

Junk markets

Strasse des 17 Juni, near Tiergarten S-Bahn station and not far
from the Victory Column
Sat. and Sun. 7 a.m.–4 p.m.

Flea-market, Nollendorfplatz

Near the National Gallery on the Reichpietschufer, between
Potsdam Bridge and the harbour on the Landwehrkanal
Sat. and Sun. 8 a.m.–3 p.m.

See A to Z, Kreuzberg   Picture market

Motoring – breakdown services (Autohilfe)

Allgemeiner Deutscher Automobil-Club (ADAC)   Automobile clubs in West
Bundesallee 29–20, Wilmersdorf; tel. 86 86–5 (information)   Berlin
Outside office hours calls are taken by the Road Patrol and
Information Centre at the Dreilinden frontier control post

Automobilclub von Deutschland (AvD),
Berlin 30, Wittenbergplatz 1; tel. 2 13 30 33

Berliner Motorclub,
Johannesthaler Chausse 333, Tel. 6044085

Allgemeiner Deutscher Motorsportverband (ADMV),   Automobile Club, East Berlin
Charlottenstrasse 60, Berlin-Mitte; tel. 2 07 19 31

ADAC-Stadtpannendienst; tel. 19211   Breakdown assistance in
AvD-Verkehrshilfsdienst; tel. 2 13 30 33   West Berlin
VMCD-Verkehrs-Hilfe; tel. 3 31 80 08

147

Practical Information

VEB Kombinat Auto Berlin,
Siegfriedstrasse 49–53; tel. 5 59 25 00
Tow-away service; open 24 hours a day

Motorways (Autobahnen)

See Highways

Museums (Museen)

West Berlin

The monthly periodical "Berlin Programm" gives a good general survey of the museums of West Berlin. It contains a section "Sights, Museums and Palaces" with the buildings listed in alphabetical order.

All the national museums associated with the Prussian Cultural Heritage Foundation (Preussischer Kulturbesitz) are closed on 1 January. The Charlottenburg Museums are also closed on Maundy Thursday.

Anti-Kriegs-Museum (anti-war museum),
Wedding, Genter Strasse 9,
Open daily 4–8 p.m.

Antiquities, Museum of
(see A to Z)

Applied Art, Museum of
(see A to Z)

Art Library
(see A to Z)

Bauhaus Archives (Bauhaus-Archiv),
Klingelhöfer Strasse 13–14
Open Mon. and Wed.–Sun. 11 a.m.–5 p.m

Belvedere
(see A to Z, Charlottenburg Palace)

Berlin Film Museum,
Grossbeerenstrasse 47
Historic films: Wed., 7 p.m.–11 p.m. Sat. 6 p.m.–11 p.m.

Berlin Museum
(see A to Z)

Berlin National Art Gallery,
Budapester Strasse 46
Open Tue.–Sun. 10 a.m.–6 p.m., Wed. 10 a.m.–10 p.m.

Berlin Panopticum,
Kurfürstendamm 227–228
Open daily 10 a.m.–11 p.m.

Botanical Museum
(see A to Z, Botanic Gardens)

Bauhaus Archives

Bröhan Museum
(see A to Z)

Brücke Museum
(see A to Z)

Charlottenburg Museums
(see A to Z, Charlottenburg Palace)

Communal Museum of Local Urban History,
(Wilmersdorf), Hohenzollerndamm 177
Open Mon.–Fri. 10 a.m.–6 p.m.

Dahlem Museums
(see A to Z)

Düppel Museum Village (Museumsdorf Düppel),
Clauertstrasse (Zehlendorf-Süd S-Bahn Station)
Reconstruction of a medieval settlement (13th c.) above the
original excavation site

East Asian Museum
(see A to Z, Dahlem Museums)

Egyptian Museum
(see A to Z)

Ethnography, Museum of
(see A to Z, Dahlem Museums)

Practical Information

Gas Lamps, Museum of (Gaslaternen-Freilichtmuseum),
(open-air museum)
Joseph-Haydn-Strasse (No. 23 bus)

German Folk Museum (Museum für Deutsche Volkskunde),
Im Winkel 6–8, Dahlem

Hunting Museum
(see A to Z, Grunewald Hunting Lodge)

Indian Art, Museum of
(see A to Z, Dahlem Museums)

Islamic Art, Museum of
(see A to Z, Dahlem Museums)

Junior Museum,
Lansstrasse 8
Open Tue.–Sun. 9 a.m.–5 p.m.
(part of the Museum of Ethnology)

Kolbe Museum (Georg-Kolbe-Museum),
Sensburger Allee 25
Open daily 10 a.m.–5 p.m., closed Mon.

Musical Instrument Museum
(see A to Z)

National Gallery
(see A to Z, New National Gallery)

Pfaueninsel Castle
(see A to Z, Pfaueninsel)

Picture Gallery
(see A to Z, Dahlem Museums)

Plaster Moulding Museum,
Sophie-Charlotte-Strasse 17–18
Open Mon.–Fri. 9 a.m.–4 p.m.

Plötzensee Memorial
(see A to Z)

Postal and Telecommunications Museum (Post- und Fern-
meldemuseum),
Urania
Open Tue.–Fri. 10 a.m.-4 p.m. Sat. and Sun. 10 a.m.-1 p.m.;
closed on public holidays
Postal history, philately, telegraphy, radio and television;
special exhibitions; film presentations on Sundays at 11 a.m.

Prehistory, Museum of
(see A to Z, Charlottenburg Palace)

Print Cabinet
(see A to Z, Dahlem Museums)

Radio Museum
(see A to Z)

Reinickendorf Local Museum (Heimatmuseum),
Alt-Hermsdorf 35
Open Wed.–Sun. 10 a.m.–6 p.m.,
closed on public holidays

Schinkel Pavilion
(see A to Z, Charlottenburg Palace)

Schöneberg Local Museum (Heimatmuseum),
Grunewaldstrasse 6–7, Berlin 62
Open Mon. and Fri. 10 a.m.–2 p.m. Thurs. 4–8 p.m.

Sculpture Gallery
(see A to Z, Dahlem Museums)

Spandau Citadel
(see A to Z)

Spandau Local Museum (Heimatmuseum)
(see A to Z, Spandau Citadel)

Tegel Palace
(see A to Z)

Museum of Transport and Technology
(under construction)
Trebbiner Strasse 9, Kreuzberg
Open Tue.–Fri. 9 a.m.–6 p.m., Sat. and Sun. 10 a.m.–6 p.m.

The old Museum of Transport and Construction (especially
railways), in the former Hamburg Station in Moabit, was
handed over by the DDR to the West Berlin authorities at the
beginning of 1984. It is at present not open to the public.

Zehlendorf Local Museum (Heimatmuseum),
Clayallee 355
Open Thu. 4–6.30 p.m.

Academy of Arts   East Berlin
(see A to Z)

Applied Art, Museum of
(see A to Z, Köpenick Palace)

Bertolt-Brecht-Haus,
Chausseestrasse 125, Berlin-Mitte
Open Tue.–Fri. 10 a.m.–noon, Thu. also 5–7 p.m., Sat. 9.30–
11.30 a.m. and 12.30–2 p.m.

Bode Museum
(see A to Z)

Brandenburg Museum (Märkisches Museum),
Am Köllnischen Park 5
Open Wed. and Sun. 9 a.m.–6 p.m., Thur. and Sat. 9 a.m.–5 p.m.
Fri. 9 a.m.–4 p.m.

Coins and Medals, Cabinet of
(see A to Z, Bode Museum)

Egyptian Museum
(see A to Z, Bode Museum)

Folk Museum
(see A to Z, Pergamon Museum)

German History, Museum of
(see A to Z, Arsenal)

Huguenot Museum
(see A to Z, Platz der Akademie)

Islamic Museum
(see A to Z, Pergamon Museum)

Köpenick Local History Gallery,
Elckener Platz 8
Open Tue. 9 a.m.–6 p.m.

Mahlsdorf Museum,
Hultschiner Damm 333
Open Sun. 11 a.m.–1 p.m.
Furniture from last quarter of 19th c.

Military Museum
(see Potsdam, Sanssouci, New Garden)

Otto-Nagel-Haus,
Märkisches Ufer 16–18
Open Sun. and Thur. 10 a.m.–6 p.m.,
Wed. 10 a.m.–10 p.m.
Revolutionary proletarian art

National Gallery
(see A to Z)

Natural History Museum (Museum für Naturkunde),
Invalidenstrasse, Berlin-Mitte
Open Tue.–Sun. 9.30 a.m.–5 p.m.
With Mineralogical Museum, Geological and Palaeontological
Museum and Zoological Museum

Neuer Marstall,
Marx-Engels Platz 7
Open Wed.–Sat. 10 a.m.–6 p.m.
Exhibitions of the Academy of Art

Old Museum
(see A to Z)

Pergamon Museum
(see A to Z)

Postal Museum
(see A to Z)

Prehistory, Museum of
(see A to Z, Bode Museum)

Robert-Koch-Museum,
Clara Zetkin Strasse 96
Open Mon.–Fri. 9 a.m.–4 p.m.

Western Asian Museum
(see A to Z, Pergamon Museum)

Music

Opera House; tel. 3 41 44 49
(see A to Z, West Berlin)

Opera and ballet

Theater des Westens,
Kantstrasse 12, Berlin 12; tel. 3 12 10 22
Reservations office open 11 a.m.–7 p.m., Sun. 3–7 p.m.

Operettas and musicals

ICC Berlin,
Messedamm; tel. 30 38–1

For information about performances tel. 11 56.

Concerts

Academy of Arts (Akademie der Künste),
Hanseatenweg 10

Radio House (Haus des Rundfunks),
Masurenallee 8–14

College of the Arts (Hochschule der Künste),
Hardenbergstrasse 33

Great Hall of National Library (Staatsbibliothek),
Potsdamer Strasse 35

Philharmonic Hall
(see A to Z)

Municipal Conservatoire (Städtisches Konservatorium),
Bundesallee 1–12

For information tel. 31 08 01 (Mon.–Fri. 8 a.m.–4 p.m.)

Music in churches

Heilandskirche,
Thusneldaallee, Tiergarten

Emperor Frederick Memorial Church
(see A to Z)
Information: tel. 3 91 13 01

Emperor William Memorial Church
(see A to Z)
Information: tel. 24 50 23

Matthäuskirche,
Schlosstrasse 44, Steglitz

Sühne-Christi-Kirche,
Torplerstrasse 1, Charlottenburg

Opera House
(see A to Z, East Berlin)

East Berlin

Haus der Deutsch-Sowjetischen Freundschaft,
Unter den Linden
Chamber concerts

Comic Opera (Komische Oper),
Behrensstrasse 55
Opera and ballet

Metropol Theater,
Friedrichstrasse 101
Operettas and musicals

Schauspielhaus,
Platz der Akademie
Orchestral concerts etc.

Schloss Friedrichsfelde,
Tierpark
Chamber concerts

Newspapers and periodicals (Zeitungen, Zeitschriften) – selection

Dailies	"Berliner Morgenpost", Kochstrasse 50
	"BZ", Kochstrasse 50
	"Tagesspiegel", Potsdamer Strasse 77–79
	"Tageszeitung", Wattstrasse 11–12
Periodicals	"Berlin-Programm", Hohenzollerndamm 89
	Local interest, What's on
	"tip-Magazin", Potsdamer Strasse 96
	Entertainments, What's on
	"zitty", Schlüterstrasse 39
	Local interest, What's on

Night life (Nachtleben)

Discothèques

Big Apple, Bundesallee 13
Big Eden, Kurfürstendamm 202
Candy, Kurfürstendamm 218
Metropol, Nollendorfplatz 5
Riverboat, Hohenzollerndamm 174

Cabarets

CaDeWe (Cabaret des Westens), Gneisenaustrasse 2;
tel. 6 91 50 99
Kabarett Klimperkasten, Otto-Suhr-Allee 100; tel. 3 13 70 07
Die Stachelschweine, Europa-Center; tel. 2 61 47 95
Die Wühlmäuse, Lietzenburger Strasse/corner of Nürnberger
Strasse 33; tel. 2 13 70 47

Bars, beer-houses

Artists' Bar "Franz Diener", Grolmanstrasse 47
Beiz, Schlüterstrasse 38
Dorfschänke Tante Anna, Joachim-Friedrich-Strasse 45
Jahrmarkt, Bleibtreustrasse 49
Joe's Bierhaus, Theodor-Heuss-Platz 12

Ku'dorf, Joachimstaler Strasse 14
Mommsen-Eck, Mommsenstrasse 45
Spree-Athen, Leibnizstrasse 60
Wendel, Richard-Wagner-Strasse 57

Blues Café, Kornerstrasse 11   Bars with music
Dublin Lounge, Hauptstrasse 85
Eierschale, Podbielskiallee at the U-Bahn station
Folkpub, Leibnizstrasse 56
Glass House, Spandauer Damm 90
Go in, Bleibtreustrasse 17
Irish Harp Pub, Giesebrechtstrasse 15
Jazzkeller, Breitenbachplatz 5
Joe's Bierhaus, Theodor-Heuss Platz 12
Loretta im Garten, Liezenburger Strasse 89
Quartier Latin, Potsdamer Strasse 96
Quasimodo, Kantstrasse 12a
Ratskeller Schmargendorf, Berkaer Platz 1
Ray's Irish Bar, Nordufer 14
Reggae Keller, Reichenberger Strasse 9
Sudhaus, Stromstrasse 11–17
Suppenkaspar, Motzstrasse 63

Baronet-Stube, Kurfurstendamm 190   Night clubs, bars, pubs
Biergarten in der Sperlingsgasse, Lietzenburger Strasse 82
Big Apple, Bundesallee 13
Bristol Bar, Kurfurstendamm 27
Buccaneer, Rankestrasse 32
Cabaret Chez Nous, Marburger Strasse 14
Dorett-Bar, Fasanenstrasse 74
Dublin, Hauptstrasse 85
Go In, Bleibtreustrasse 17
Harp Irish Pub, Giesebrechtstrasse 15
Hasenstall, Kurfurstendamm 34
Irish Pub, Europa Centre
King's Pub, Kurfurstendamm 210
Kleine Bar, Schaperstrasse 12
Komma, Pfalzburger Strasse 10
La Vie en Rose, Europa Centre
Medly-Club, Buckower Damm 232
Moore's Irish Pub, Kantstrasse 91
New Eden Saloon, Kurfürstendamm 71
Pianoforte-Bar, Wittenbergplatz 5
Quartier Latin, Potdamer Strasse 99
Scotch-Club, Marburger Strasse 15
The Original Irish Pub, Eisenacher Strasse 6
Union Jack, Schluterstrasse 15

Diener, Grolmannstrasse 47   Pinten ("dives")
Kleine Weltlaterne, Nestorstrasse 10
Ku'dorf, Joachimstaler Strasse 15
Loretta im Garten, Lietzenburger Strasse 89
Pfeffermühle, Pfalzburger Strasse 4
Zur Nolle, Nollendorfplatz U-Bahn Station

Ambiente, Mommsenstrasse 9   Celebrity haunts
AxBax, Leibnizstrasse 34
Exil, Paul-Lincke-Ufer 44a
Fofi, Fasanenstrasse 70
Heinz Holl, Damaschkestrasse 26

Practical Information

	Kempinskis Bristol-Bar, Kurfürstendamm 27
	Paris Bar, Kantstrasse 152
Casino	Casino (Spielbank), Europa-Center (second floor)
Dancing	Buccaneer, Rankestrasse 32
	Café des Westens, Kurfürstendamm 227
	Bristol Bar, Kurfürstendamm 15
	Inter-Continental, Budapester Strasse 2
	Ballhaus Lustige Witwe, Alt-Moabit 55
	Ballhaus Tiergarten, Perleberger Strasse 62
	Café Keese, Bismarckstrasse 108
	Tanz-Palast, Kurfürstendamm 22
	V.I.P. Club, Europa-Center (20th floor)
	Yesterday, Tauentzienstrasse 8
Transvestite haunts	Chez Nous, Marburger Strasse 14
	Lützower Lampe, Behaimstrasse 21
	Romy Haag, Welserstrasse 24 (corner of Fuggerstrasse)
Bars in East Berlin	Hafenbar, Chausseestrasse 20
	Lindencorso, Unter den Linden/corner of Friedrichstrasse
	Moskwa-Bar, Karl-Marx-Allee
	Operncafe (Nachtbar)
Discothèques in East Berlin	Cafe Friedrichstadt (Pudelbar), Friedrichstrasse 112a
	Disco 11, Franzosische Strasse 47
	Jucca, Wisbyer/corner of Anettestrasse
	Kleine Melodie, Friedrichstrasse 127
	Lolott, Schonhauser Allee 46a
	Pinguin Bar, Luxemburgstrasse 9

Opening times (Öffnungszeiten)

Banks	See that entry
Museums	See that entry
Post offices	See Postal services
Shops	Shops are usually open from 9 a.m. to 6 p.m. Monday to Friday and from 9 a.m. to 1 p.m. on Saturdays. Department stores close at 6.30 p.m. Monday to Friday and 2 p.m. on Saturdays. On the first Saturday in the month shops and department stores in the main shopping streets stay open until 6 p.m.
	The following shops have longer opening hours:
Food shops	Edeka, Schlosstrasse U-Bahn Station
	Open Mon.–Fri. 3 p.m.–10 p.m., Sat. 1 p.m.–10 p.m., Sun. and public holidays 10 a.m.–8 p.m.
	Métro, Fehrbelliner Platz U-Bahn Station
	Open daily midday–10.30 p.m.
	Métro, Kurfürstendamm U-Bahn Station
	Open Mon.–Fri. and Sun. 5 p.m.–11 p.m., Sat. 5 p.m.–midnight
Flowers	Zoo Station
	Open Mon.–Sat. 8 a.m.–8 p.m., Sun. 9 a.m.–6 p.m.

Tegel Airport
Open daily 8 a.m.–8 p.m.

Zoo Station
Open daily 5.30 a.m.–10.30 p.m.
Tegel Airport
Open daily 5 a.m.–9 p.m.
Kiosk W. Wiedenberg, Kurfürstendamm (corner of Joachim-
staler Strasse)
Open Mon.–Fri. 6 a.m.–9.30 p.m., Sat. 7 a.m.–10 p.m., Sun.
8 a.m.–9.30 p.m.

Hairdressing establishments are closed on Mondays; on other
weekdays they have normal shop hours.

Pharmacies (Apotheken)

Information about pharmacists providing out-of-hours services can be obtained by dialling 1141. The names of
pharmacists providing such services are also posted up in
pharmacies and (in West Berlin) police stations.

Postal services

Post offices in Berlin are normally open Monday to Friday from
8 a.m. to 6 p.m., Sat. from 8 a.m. to 12 noon. A number of offices
have longer hours:

Zoo Station; tel. 3 13 97 99
Open night and day. General delivery letters marked
"bahnhofspostlagernd" can be collected here.

Postamt 519 (Tegel Airport); tel. 43 08–523
Open daily 6.30 a.m.–9 p.m.

Post office in International Congress Centre
Open Mon.–Fri. 9 a.m.–1 p.m., 1.45–4 p.m.

Post office in Tegel Airport
Open daily 6.30 a.m.–9 p.m.

Post office in International Congress Centre
Open Mon.–Fri. 9 a.m.–1 p.m. and 1.45–4 p.m.

Postamt 301, Marburger Strasse 12
Normal opening hours

Public transport (Öffentliche Verkehrsmittel)

The S-Bahn (suburban railway system) in West Berlin was
handed over by the Reichsbahn (East Berlin state railway) to
the West Berlin BVG at the beginning of 1984. There are three
lines:

An Underground train on an above-ground stretch of track

S1 Anhalter Bahnhof–Wannsee
S2 Lichtenrade–Frohnau
S3 Friedrichstrasse–Wannsee.

U-Bahn

The U-Bahn (subway) is run by the West Berlin municipal transport organisation, Berliner Verkehrs-Betriebe (BVG). The system has a total length of 106·3 km (66 miles) and a total of about 1000 cars. Trains run at intervals of 5–10 minutes during the rush hours and 10–15 minutes at other times.

There are eight lines in operation:
Line 1: Ruhleben–Zoo–Schlesisches Tor
Line 2: Krumme Lanke–Wittenbergplatz
Line 3: Uhlandstrasse–Kurfürstendamm–Wittenbergplatz
Line 4: Innsbrucker Platz–Bayerischer Platz–Nollendorfplatz
(Line 5 closed down)
Line 6: Tegel – six stations in East Berlin, stopping at Friedrichstrasse–Alt-Mariendorf
Line 7: Rathaus Spandau–Rudow
Line 8: Osloer Strasse – six stations in East Berlin without stopping – Leinestrasse/Neukölln
Line 9: Osloer Strasse–Zoo–Kurfürstendamm–Rathaus Steglitz

Magnetic railway

At present under test.

Buses

Berlin has a dense network of bus routes, also run by BVG.

Tourist tickets

BVG offer visitors a tourist ticket (Touristenkarte) covering unlimited travel for either 2 or 4 days on all BVG transport

(U-Bahn, buses, Kladow-Wannsee ferry on Stern- und Kreisschiffahrt boats) except bus excursion and special services.

Tickets can be bought at the following offices:

BVG ticket office, Kleistpark U-Bahn Station

BVG-Kiosk Zoo,
Hardenbergplatz

BVG-Kiosk Spandau,
Altstadter Ring

ZOB Travel Agency at Central Bus Station,
Masurenallee 4–6

Reisebüro Ehlert,
Martin-Luther-Strasse 103

Theatre Reservations Office in KaDeWe

Ticket offices in the Kurt-Schumacher-Platz and Zoo U-Bahn stations and season ticket offices at some other stations

BVG; tel. 2165088.   Information

Restaurants

Alte Fischerhutte, Fisherhüttenweg   Garden and country
Alter Fritz, Tegeler Forst   restaurants
Blockhaus Nikolskoe, Wannsee
Chalet Suisse, Königin-Luise-Strasse/Im Jagen 5
Cour Carrée, Savignyplatz 6
Eierschale, Podbielskiallee 50
Grunewaldturm, Havelchaussee
Haus Zur Linde, Alt Gatow 1–3
Hundekehle, Hundekehlestrasse 33
Joe Beau, Lais Delbrückstrasse 37
Pavillon Stölpchensee, Wannsee
Schildhornbaude, Havelchaussee, Schildhorn
Seeterrasse Tegel, Wilkestrasse 1
Seepavillon Tegel, Tegelort
Strandbaude, Glieniker See
Waldhaus, Am Grunewaldturm
Wannsee-Terrassen, Wannseebadweg
Zum lustigen Finken, Alt-Lübars 20

Alt-Berliner Schneckenhaus, Kurfürstendamm 37   Restaurants
Alter Krug Dahlem, Königin-Luise-Strasse 52 (one of the
oldest village inns in Berlin)
Ax Bax, Leibnizstrasse 34
Bierpinsel, Schloss Strasse 17
Dorfgasthaus, Sächsische Strasse 7
Du Pont, Budapester Strasse 1
Esstaurant, Windscheidstrasse 40
Funkturm-Restaurant (in Radio Tower; at 55 m (180 ft))

Practical Information

Glasmenagerie, Martin-Luther-Strasse 47
Hardke, Meinekestrasse 27
Heinz Holl, Damaschkestrasse 26 (frequented by artists)
Heising, Rankestrasse 32 (open from 7 p.m.)
Historische Gaststätte auf der Zitadelle (inn on Spandau Citadel)
Jahrmarkt, Bleibtreustrasse 49
Laube, Horstweg 2
Luise, Königin-Luise-Strasse 40
Mampes Gute Stube, Kurfürstendamm 14 (old Berlin inn)
Mövenpick, Europa Centre
Nantes Bierecke, Droysenstrasse 1
Pam Pam, Xantener Strasse 9
Pullman, Messedamm 11 (ICC)
*Ritz, Rankestrasse 36 (specialities from many countries)
Rockendorf's Restaurant, Dusterhauptstrasse 1
Schöneberger Weltlaterne, Motzstrasse 61
Silberterrasse im KaDeWe, Tauentzienstrasse 21
Suppenkaspar, Motzstrasse 63
Universum, Kurfürstendamm 153
Waldhaus, Onkel-Tom-Strasse 50
Wertheim-Grillroom, Kurfürstendamm 231
Zille-Eck, Sophie-Charlotte-Strasse 88

Wine-houses	Alter Krug Dahlem. Königin-Luise-Strasse 52
	Besenwirtschaft, Uhlandstrasse 159
	Habel-Weinstube, Hohenzollerndamm 93
	Hardy an der Oper, Zauritzweg 9
	Historischer Weinkeller, Alt Pichelsdorf 32 (historic wine cellar at Spandau)
	Kamin-Weinstuben, Fasanenstrasse 15
	Kurpfalz, Wilmersdorfer Strasse 93
	Pfälzer Weinstuben, Fasanenstrasse 78
	Weinrestaurant Bernhard Heising, Rankestrasse 32
	Weinstube am Schlossparktheater, Wrangelstrasse 11
	Weinkrüger, Kurfürstendamm 25
	Wiener Stüberl, Giesebrechtstrasse 3
	Zwiwwel, Bruchsaler Strasse 6 (at the RIAS)
Austrian	Ambiente, Mommsenstrasse 9
	Hühner Hugo, Brandenburgische Strasse 33
Bohemian and Hungarian	Böhmisches Landhaus, Landhausstrasse 31
	Orangerie, Konstanzer Strasse 1 (corner of Xantener Strasse)
	Schipkapass, Hohenzollerndamm 185
	Schwejk, Prager Gasthaus (Prague Inn), Ansbacher Strasse 4
	Zlata Praha, Meinekestrasse 4
Chinese	China Garten, Messedamm 10
	Hongkong, Kurfürstendamm 210
	Kowloon, Klosterstrasse 36 (Spandau)
	Lee-Wah, Kurfürstendamm 92
	Lotos House, Bismarckstrasse 23
	Lung Fung, Wittenbergplatz 4
	Shanghai, Bleibtreustrasse 31
	Tai-Tung, Budapester Strasse 50
Egyptian	Pompei, Konigstrasse 44
	Restaurant am Nil, Kaiserdamm 114

Alt-Luxemburg, Pestalozzistrasse 70	French
Bistroquet, Uhlandstrasse 49	
Chalet Corniche, Königsallee 5b	
Chapeau Claque, Damaschkestrasse 21	
Coq d'Or, Dahlmannstrasse 20	
Du Pont, Budapester Strasse 1	
Ganymed, Fasanenstrasse 65	
Grille, Kurfürstendamm 202	
La Provence, Schlüterstrasse 67	
La Puce, Schillerstrasse 20	
Le Bou Bou, Kurfürstendamm 190	
Le Paris, Kurfürstendamm 211 (corner of Uhlandstrasse)	
Tunnel, Kurfürstendamm 190	
Akropolis, Wielandstrasse 38	Greek
Lissos, Pfalzburger Strasse 83	
Olympia, Jochimstaler Strasse 30	
Tatavla, Mommsenstrasse 10 (corner of Schlüterstrasse)	
Taverna Plaka, Joachimstaler Strasse 14	
Ashoka Taj, Leibnizstrasse 12	Indian
Kalkutta, Bleibtreustrasse 17	
Java, Nestorstrasse 6	Indonesian
Petit Chinois, Spandauer Damm 82	
Anselmo, Damaschkestrasse 17	Italian
Bacco, Marburger Strasse 5	
Borbone, Windscheidstrasse 14	
Don Camillo, Schloss Strasse 7–8	
Il Sorriso, Kurfürstenstrasse 76	
La Piazza, Savignyplatz 13	
La Vernaccia, Am Breitenbachplatz 4	
Mantovani, Uhlandstrasse 29	
Daitokai, Tauentzienstrasse 9–12	Japanese
Kyoto, Wilmersdorfer Strasse 94 (near Adenauerplatz)	
Jüdisches Gemeindehaus, Fasanenstrasse 79	Jewish (kosher)
Kibbuz, Otto-Suhr-Allee 25	
Mifgash Israel, Nachodstrasse 24 (near Bundesallee)	
Krakowiak, Nürnberger Strasse 14	Polish
Staropolska, Bismarckstrasse 100	
Mazurka, Lietzenburger Strasse 74	Russian
Käsekiste, Europa-Center	Scandinavian
Kopenhagen, Kurfürstendamm 203	
Borriquito, Wielandstrasse/Kantstrasse	Spanish and Portuguese
Casa Algarvia, Goethestrasse 61	
El Bodegón, Schlüterstrasse 61	
El Pepito, Kantstrasse 134	
Goya, Bismarckstrasse 28	
La Mancha, Bismarckstrasse 77	
Mallorca Express, Schlüterstrasse/corner of Kantstrasse	
Olé, Droysenstrasse 10	

Practical Information

Swiss	Chalet Suisse, Königin-Luise-Strasse/Im Jagen 5 Tessiner Stuben, Bleibtreustrasse 33 Walliser Stuben, Lietzenburger Strasse 79
Turkish and Oriental	Istanbul, Knesebeckstrasse 77 Mustafa-Grill, Kaiser-Friedrich-Strasse 61a
Vegetarian	Lebensbaum, Pfalzburger Strasse 20 Verena, Kurfürstendamm 67
Yugoslav	Adria, Kurfürstendamm 207 Adriatic Grill, Kurfürstendamm 96 Boka, Fasanenstrasse 73 Bosna-Grill, Bundesallee 93 Galaja, Otto-Suhr-Allee 139 Novo Skopje, Kurfürstendamm 38 Split Grill, Blucherplatz 2
Restaurants in East Berlin	Budapest, Karl-Marx-Allee 90 (Hungarian) Bukarest, Frankfurter Allee 13 (Romanian) Fernsehturm (television tower), Alexanderplatz Mazurka, Klement-Gottwald-Allee 179 Morava, Rathausstrasse 5 (Czech) Moskau, Karl-Marx-Allee 34 (Russian) Palast der Republik (several restaurants) Ratskeller (in the Town Hall) Sofia, Leipziger Strasse 46 (Bulgarian) Tarnovo, Hermann-Dunker-Strasse Haus Warschau, Karl-Marx-Allee 93 (fish) Wernergruner Bierstuben, Karl-Liebknecht-Strasse 11 Zur letzten Instanz, Waisenstrasse 14–16
Weinstuben in East Berlin	Adria, Friedrichstrasse 134 Alt-Cöllner Schankstuben, Friedrichsgracht 50 Ermelerhaus, Märkisches Ufer 10-12 Ganymed, Schiffbauerdamm 5 Historische Weinstuben, Poststrasse 23 Schoppenstube, Chausseestrasse 110

Sightseeing tours

City tours	Berolina Sightseeing Tours, Kurfürstendamm 25; tel. 8 83 31 31
	Severin & Kühn, Kurfürstendamm 216; tel. 8 83 10 15
	BBS (Berliner Bären Stadtrundfahrten), Ecke Kurfürstenda, Tel. 2134077
	These firms run daily sightseeing tours of West Berlin, night-club excursions (inclusive charge covering admission, food, drinks and sightseeing), combined tours of West and East Berlin (passport necessary) and special trips visiting museums.
Potsdam	Although Potsdam lies so close to West Berlin it is not easy to get there, particularly for West Germans. Foreign visitors can, however, visit it on a half-day or day tour arranged by a travel

agency (passport required). The tours are run daily in summer and three times a week in winter. They include a drive round the town and a walk through the park with visits to Sanssouci and Cäcilienhof.

See entry   Boat trips

Sport

Berlin offers excellent facilities for all kinds of sport. For winter sports enthusiasts there are toboggan-runs, skiing-slopes and ice-rinks.
For information about sports facilities and sporting events apply to the Landessportbund Berlin, Jesse-Owens-Allee 2, tel. 30002-0.

Stations (Bahnhöfe)

The only station for long-distance trains in West Berlin is the Zoo Station; inter-zone trains also stop at Berlin-Wannsee.   West Berlin

Ostbahnhof (formerly Schlesischer Bahnhof) Friedrichstrasse Station.   East Berlin

Swimming-pools

Freibad Halensee, Königsallee 5a   West Berlin
Freibad Jungfernheide, Volkspark
Freibad Lübars
Freibad Oberhavel, Havelschanze 27–31
Freibad Plötzensee, Nordufer 24
Freibad Tegelsee, Schwarzer Weg (facilities for naturists)
Strandbad Wannsee, Wannseebadweg (facilities for naturists)
Club-Badeparadies, Buschkrugallee 64

Müggelsee, Fürstenwalder Damm 838   Swimming-pools in East
Grünau, at Sports Monument, Regatta Strasse   Berlin
Orankesee, Hohenschönhausen, Gertrudstrasse
Friedrichshagen, Müggelseedamm 216
Pankow, Schlosspark, Wolfshagener Strasse
Monbijou Park (children's swimming-pool)

Taxis

There are some 100 taxi-phones and 350 taxi ranks in Berlin.
The fare is made up of a basic charge and a rate per kilometre.
There is no difference between day and night tariffs.
To call a taxi, ring 69 02, 26 10 26, 21 60 60 or 24 02 02.

Theatres

State theatres

Schiller-Theater,
Bismarckstrasse 110

Schiller-Theater-Werkstatt,
Bismarckstrasse 110
Theatre Workshop (experimental theatre)

Schlosspark-Theater,
Schlosstrasse 48

Privately owned theatres

Berliner Kammerspiele/Theater der Jugend,
Alt-Moabit 99

Freie Theateranstalt Berlin,
Klausenerplatz 19

Freie Volksbühne,
Schaperstrasse 24
Classical and modern plays

Hansa-Theater,
Alt-Moabit 48
Dialect folk plays

Hebbel-Theater,
Stresemannstrasse 29

Junges Theater
Friesenstrasse 14

Kleines Theater,
Südwestkorso 64

Komödie,
Kurfürstendamm 206

Ratibor-Theater,
Ratiborstrasse 10
Experimental theatre

Renaissance-Theater,
Hardenbergstrasse 6
Straight plays and comedies

Schaubühne,
Kurfürstendamm 153 (Lehniner Platz)
Modern and experimental plays

Theater am Kreuzberg,
Möckernstrasse 66

Theater am Kurfürstendamm,
Kurfürstendamm 206
Straight plays and comedies

Theater des Westens,
Kantstrasse 12

Theatermanufaktur,
Hallesches Ufer 32
Plays on contemporary issues

Theater Zentrifuge,
in Künstlerhaus Bethanien,
Mariannenplatz 2

Tribüne,
Otto-Suhr-Allee 18
Straight plays and comedies

Vaganten-Bühne,
Kantstrasse 12a
Straight plays, modern theatre

Zan-Pollo-Theater,
Rheinstrasse 45

Zaubertheater im Karree,
Kurfürstendamm 206

Birne,
Assmannshauser Strasse 12

Theatres for children and
young people

Fliegendes Theater,
Gneisenaustrasse 2 (Mehringhof)

Grips,
Altonaer Strasse 22

Rote Grütze,
Mehringdamm 51

Schaubühne,
Kurfürstendamm 153

UFA-Fabrik,
Viktoriastrasse 13

Klecks Berliner Kindertheater mit Puppen,
Schinkestrasse 8–9

Puppet theatres

Literarisches Figurentheater "die bühne",
Urania,
Kleiststrasse 14

Berliner Ensemble,
Bertolt-Brecht-Platz
Modern plays, Brecht

Theatres in East Berlin

Deutsches Theater,
Schumannstrasse 13a
Classical and modern plays

Kammerspiele,
Schumannstrasse 13a
Classical and modern plays and comedies

Practical Information

Maxim-Gorki-Theater,
Am Festungsgraben 2
Straight plays

Theater im Palast,
Marx-Engels-Platz

Volksbühne,
Rosa-Luxemburg-Platz
Straight plays

Theatre for young people   Theater der Freundschaft,
Pettenkoferstrasse 4 and Parkaue Lichtenberg
Socialist plays for young people

Cabaret and variety   Die Distel 1,
Friedrichstrasse 101

Die Distel 2,
Degnerstrasse 9

Friedrichstadt-Palast,
Friedrichstrasse 134
Opened in 1984, large auditorium seating 1800, Kleine Revue
with 250 seats, night show

Puppet theatre   Puppentheater Berlin,
Greifswalder Strasse 81

Travel documents (Reisedokumente)

Foreign visitors travelling to West Berlin by air require the same
documents as for West Germany: i.e. for visitors from Western
countries normally only a standard passport (not a British
Visitor's Passport). West Germans require only an identity card.
Visitors travelling by car require a passport and the usual car
papers. Transit visas for the journey through the German
Democratic Republic are issued at the frontier.
For entry into East Berlin see East Berlin, Entry into.

Universities (Universitäten)

West Berlin   Free University
(see A to Z)

University of Technology (Technische Universität),
Hardenbergstrasse 34, Charlottenburg
Formed in 1879 by the amalgamation of the Academy of
Building (Bauakademie), founded in 1799, and the Industrial
Academy (Gewerbeakademie), founded in 1821.

East Berlin   Humboldt University
(see A to Z)

Youth hostels (Jugendherbergen)

Reservations can be made through Deutsches Jugendherberg-swerk, Landesverband Berlin, Geschäftsstelle Bayernalle 35; tel. 3 05 30 55
West Berlin

CVJM-Haus,
Einemstrasse 10, Berlin 62 (Schöneberg), 80 beds

Jugendgästehaus am Wannsee,
Kronprinzessinnenweg 27 (Nikolasee), 264 beds

Jugendgästehaus Berlin,
Kluckstrasse 3, Berlin 30 (Tiergarten), 420 beds

Jugendherberge Bayernallee,
Bayernallee 36, Berlin 19 (Charlottenburg), 104 beds

Jugendherberge Ernst Reuter,
Hermsdorfer Damm 48, Berlin 26 (Hermsdorf), 136 beds

Jugendhotel Bellevue Tower,
Linkstrasse 32, Berlin 30 (Tiergarten), 144 beds

Studentenhotel,
Meininger Strasse 10, Berlin 62 (Schöneberg), 180 beds

Jugendtouristenhotel "Egon Schultz",
Am Tierpark, Friedrichsfelde
Youth Hostels in East Berlin

Touristenhaus für den internationalen Jugendaustausch, (house for international youth exchanges), Grünau, Bezirk Köpenick, Dahmestrasse 6

Useful Telephone Numbers at a glance

Emergencies

Police (throughout Berlin)	110
Emergency doctor, fire department (throughout Berlin)	112
Medical emergency service	31 00 31
Pharmacist (information on out-of-hours service)	1141
Poisoning advisory service	3 02 30 22
"Seelsorge" (=Samaritans)	1 11 01

Vehicle breakdowns

ADAC	86 86 1
AvD	2 13 30 33
VMCD	3 31 80 08
DRK (East Berlin)	85 85 (115)

Highway – Frontier Control Posts (Police)

Dreilinden	8 03 60 51
Heerstrasse	3 66 10 66

Motoring Organisations

ADAC	86 86–1
AvD	2 13 30 33
Berlin Motor Club	6 03 01 13

Practical Information

Airlines in West Berlin (seat reservations)
Air France	2 50 25
Austrian Air Lines	24 50 24
British Airways	69 10 21
Lufthansa	88 75–5
Pan Am	88 10 11
Scandinavian Airlines	8 71 70 71
Swissair	8 83 90 01

Airlines in East Berlin
Aeroflot	2 29 28 33
Interflug	67 20

Information
Airport Tegel	41 01–1
Berlin information centre	3 10 04–0
Bus Station at the Radio Tower	3 01 80 28
Church services	11 57
Cultural information (Festivals)	26 34–250
East Berlin, entry	
for foreigners and West Germans	8 67–1
for West Berliners	87 02 31
Municipal transport services (BVG)	2 16 50 88
Music in churches	31 08 01
Rail services, West German	3 12 10 42
Rail services, East German	3 13 30 55
Sporting events	8 91 10 71
Theatre and concert reservations	11 56
Tourist information office	2 12 34

Lost property
Police	69 91
BVG (Municipal transport)	2 16 14 13

Taxis	69 02, 26 10 26

Baedeker's Travel Guides

"The maps and illustrations are lavish. The arrangement of information (alphabetically by city) makes it easy to use the book."
— *San Francisco Examiner-Chronicle*

What's there to do and see in foreign countries? Travelers who rely on Baedeker, one of the oldest names in travel literature, will miss nothing. Baedeker's bright red, internationally recognized covers open up to reveal fascinating A-Z directories of cities, towns, and regions, complete with their sights, museums, monuments, cathedrals, castles, gardens and ancestral homes—an approach that gives the traveler a quick and easy way to plan a vacation itinerary.

And Baedekers are filled with over 200 full colour photos and detailed maps, including a full-size, fold-out roadmap for easy vacation driving. Baedeker—the premier name in travel for over 150 years.

Please send me the books checked below:

☐ **Austria** $16.95
0–13–056127–4

☐ **Caribbean** $16.95
0–13–056143–6

☐ **Costa Brava** $11.95
0–13–055880–X

☐ **Denmark** $16.95
0–13–058124–0

☐ **Egypt** $16.95
0–13–056358–7

☐ **France** $16.95
0–13–055814–1

☐ **Germany** $16.95
0–13–055830–3

☐ **Great Britain** $16.95
0–13–055855–9

☐ **Greece** $16.95
0–13–056002–2

☐ **Greek Islands** $11.95
0–13–058132–1

☐ **Ireland** $16.95
0–13–058140–2

☐ **Israel** $16.95
0–13–056176–2

☐ **Italy** $16.95
0–13–055897–4

☐ **Japan** $16.95
0–13–056382–X

☐ **Loire** $11.95
0–13–056375–7

☐ **Mediterranean Islands** $16.95
0–13–056862–7

☐ **Mexico** $16.95
0–13–056069–3

☐ **Netherlands, Belgium and Luxembourg** $16.95
0–13–056028–6

☐ **Portugal** $16.95
0–13–056135–5

☐ **Provence/Côte d'Azur** $11.95
0–13–056938–0

☐ **Rail Guide to Europe** $16.95
0–13–055971–7

☐ **Rhine** $11.95
0–13–056466–4

☐ **Scandinavia** $16.95
0–13–056085–5

☐ **Spain** $16.95
0–13–055913–X

☐ **Switzerland** $16.95
0–13–056044–8

☐ **Turkish Coast** $11.95
0–13–058173–9

☐ **Tuscany** $11.95
0–13–056482–6

☐ **Yugoslavia** $16.95
0–13–056184–3

Please turn the page for an order form and a list of additional Baedeker Guides.

A series of city guides filled with color photographs and detailed maps and floor plans from one of the oldest names in travel publishing:

Please send me the books checked below:

☐ **Amsterdam**......................$11.95
0–13–057969–6

☐ **Athens**............................$11.95
0–13–057977–7

☐ **Bangkok**..........................$11.95
0–13–057985–8

☐ **Berlin**............................$11.95
0–13–367996–9

☐ **Brussels**..........................$11.95
0–13–368788–0

☐ **Budapest**.........................$11.95
0–13–058199–2

☐ **Cologne**..........................$11.95
0–13–058181–X

☐ **Copenhagen**......................$11.95
0–13–057993–9

☐ **Florence**..........................$11.95
0–13–369505–0

☐ **Frankfurt**.........................$11.95
0–13–369570–0

☐ **Hamburg**.........................$11.95
0–13–369687–1

☐ **Hong Kong**.......................$11.95
0–13–058009–0

☐ **Istanbul**..........................$11.95
0–13–058207–7

☐ **Jerusalem**........................$11.95
0–13–058017–1

☐ **London**...........................$11.95
0–13–058025–2

☐ **Madrid**...........................$11.95
0–13–058033–3

☐ **Moscow**..........................$11.95
0–13–058041–4

☐ **Munich**...........................$11.95
0–13–370370–3

☐ **New York**.........................$11.95
0–13–058058–9

☐ **Paris**.............................$11.95
0–13–058066–X

☐ **Prague**...........................$11.95
0–13–058215–8

☐ **Rome**.............................$11.95
0–13058074–0

☐ **San Francisco**....................$11.95
0–13–058082–1

☐ **Singapore**........................$11.95
0–13–058090–2

☐ **Stuttgart**.........................$11.95
0–13–058223–9

☐ **Tokyo**............................$11.95
0–13–058108–9

☐ **Venice**............................$11.95
0–13–058116–X

☐ **Vienna**...........................$11.95
0–13–371303–2

PRENTICE HALL PRESS
Order Department—Travel Books
200 Old Tappan Road
Old Tappan, New Jersey 07675
In U.S. include $1 postage and handling for 1st book, 25¢ each additional book.
Outside U.S. $2 and 50¢ respectively.

Enclosed is my check or money order for $_____

NAME_____

ADDRESS_____

CITY_____STATE_____ZIP_____